ADVERSITY &PAIN

The Gifts That Nobody Wants

Os Hillman

ASLAN GROUP
PUBLISHING

Os Hillman

Os Hillman has had a career in marketing, advertising and publishing for over twenty years. He has owned and operated The Aslan Group Ltd., a full service advertising agency for thirteen years. During this time his firm served such clients as American Express, Steinway & Sons piano company, Peachtree Software, Parisian Department Stores, ADP payroll services, and many Christian and non-profit organizations such as the Christian Broadcasting Network, the Nazarene Denomination, and Fellowship of Companies for Christ.

In November of 1995 Os began Aslan Group Publishing, a Christian publishing company that publishes books and materials focusing on business from a Christian perspective. In March of 1995, Os launched the premier issue of *Christians IN Business* magazine, a magazine established to focus on the needs of Christian business people.

Os is author of several publications including, *The Five Fallacies of the Purposes of Money, Adversity and Pain: The Gifts Nobody Wants, and Proven Strategies for Business Success.* He is Executive Editor and Publisher of *Christians IN Business* magazine.

Os is a single parent and has one teenage daughter, Charis.

Aslan Group Publishing/*Christians In Business* magazine
3595 Webb Bridge Road, Alpharetta, Georgia 30202
770-442-1500   Fax770-442-1844
E-Mail: hillman.aslangroup@mindspring.com

Extraordinary afflictions are not always the punishment of extraordinary sins, but sometimes the trial of extraordinary graces. God hath many sharp-cutting instruments, and rough files for the polishing of His jewels; and those He especially loves, and means to make the most resplendent, He hath oftenest His tools upon.

— Archbishop Leighton

CONTENTS

Dedication

To my one and only child, Charis Rebecca Hillman, whose name means grace. May God bestow much grace throughout your life. I love you.

Acknowledgments

There have been many people who have walked the path of adversity with me over these last several years. Thank you for walking with me down these rocky paths - Lillian Hillman (my mother), Jim and Genie Mezick, Aubry Holder, Danny Ives, Bill Weaver, Ray Miller, and Eric and Nancy Mears.

I especially wish to thank Mike and Sue Dowgiewicz, who spiritually adopted me into their own family as one of theirs. Without their continued encouragement and love I could not have walked forward in the midst of these adversities.

Special thanks also to Sandy Hardy and Chris Weaver for their editorial help on this project.

Chapter 1

ENTITLEMENTS

When times are good, be happy; but when times are bad,
consider: God has made the one as well as the other
(Ecclesiastes 7:14).

The No. 1 question we all face at one time or another is this: Why does a loving God allow pain and hardship to take place in this world? Perhaps there is no other more gut-wrenching question than that for both the Christian and the non-believer. Our finite minds cannot reconcile pain and suffering with a loving God. When we go through experiences first-hand, we derive lessons and experiences that can be passed on to others. If we have walked through adversity victoriously, we can help others in ways that simply studying the subject intellectually could never accomplish. Some of the things that I've learned personally from the school of hardship may help you if you find yourself struggling in the arena of pain.

First, we must clearly grasp that—

. . . We live in a fallen world.
. . . Sin is still very much part of our lives.
. . . Satan is allowed to reign within the limits God determines.
. . . The perfect world Adam and Eve enjoyed ceased to exist when they sinned in the Garden of Eden.

We need to keep these facts in mind as we try to understand the world we live in. Suffering, disease, and hunger are givens in our world; but as we explore the role of adversity in the life of a believer, we begin to see purpose and meaning for it by light of Scripture.

First, let me say I cannot speak from experience of physical pain and suffering. My experience has been more in dealing with other emotionally painful situations related to personal and business relationships.

In March of 1994 several life-changing events occurred that dramatically changed my life. My wife of fifteen years separated from me; ultimately she would file for divorce after nearly two and a half years of separation. At that time I owned an advertising agency for thirteen years that had prospered after years of high intensity effort.

When my wife announced to me that she wanted a divorce, I was devastated. I discovered my personal circumstances would only get worse. God began peeling away every security blanket I had so carefully erected. During the first three months after my wife left me, the following other events took place:

- A client that represented 80% of our business fired us as their ad agency.

- An investment company in which we had placed $100,000 of our company cash and a large number of profit-sharing accounts and personal accounts was investigated by the Securities and Exchange Commission. Their assets were seized; our money was frozen and later lost.

- A major account we had won just two months earlier fired us because of a series of errors by our staff and vendors. I had never seen so many errors on one account. Everywhere we turned some strange thing happened, and our people did not normally make such ridiculous mistakes.

- Two clients refused to pay their balances of over $160,000 and there was no question they owed the money.

- Another investment firm in which we had entrusted company money and half of our personal assets called. One of the partners had embezzled money. They were freezing all investors' accounts in an attempt to recapture the assets. Between the two investment accounts over $300,000 had been lost.

- We won a big account only to learn two weeks later that it had been acquired by another company. They would be moving their headquarters to the West Coast and would need an agency out there.

- My vice president left the company and attempted to take our second largest account.

- Then, several months later I lost my relationship with my only daughter because of the hostile divorce situation.

I was alone, broken, and suffering. Why God?

Oh, the depth of the riches of the wisdom and
knowledge of God.
How unsearchable His judgments,
and His paths beyond tracing out!
"Who has known the mind of the Lord?
Or who has been His counselor?"
"Who has ever given to God,
that God should repay Him?"
For from Him and through Him and to Him are all things.
To Him be the glory forever! Amen
(Romans 11:33-36).

There are some events in our lives that cannot be explained adequately: "His paths are beyond tracing out! Who has known the mind of the Lord?" All we know is what Paul tells us—that ALL things are FROM Him and THROUGH Him and TO Him. No matter whether Satan or God is the source, all things that come to us pass through God's filtering system.

He is the filter. God uses the good and the bad for His refining process.

In order for us to start making sense of adversity and pain in our lives, we should first look at a presumption that most of us are guilty of when it relates to this subject of adversity.

Entitlements

We have been duped into believing that the world owes us. It owes us a good living, a loving wife or husband, good health for our whole life, intimacy on demand from our mates and paid vacations every year of our working lives. The world has told us that we are entitled to these things. The problem is, God has never said that. Dr. Chris Thurman, Christian counselor and author of *The Lies We Believe*, describes this destructive mindset as "entitlements."

> I get into a lot of trouble for this one in my counseling. I try to teach that we are not entitled to anything—we are not entitled to life, liberty and the pursuit of happiness; we're not entitled to kindness, love, respect, fair play, a decent job, a loving spouse. Now I simultaneously teach that while it's not our birthright to have those things, it's okay to want them. But there's a huge difference between a person who wants love and a person who feels entitled to it. And with clients I'll go after this all the time—the humility of wanting kindness from people versus the arrogance of demanding it and feeling owed it.
>
> In marriage, I work on this all the time with couples. I say, "Look, you guys have actually fallen into the trap of demanding that your needs get met in the marriage rather than more respectfully approaching each other wanting them to get met and knowing that if the partner doesn't meet that need that God has promised to." In this culture we have been trained not to believe this. We have in our culture what we call entitlement programs. And McDonald's—not to knock any corporation or get us in trouble—says, "You deserve a break today." And my bias is, "No, you don't deserve it; but would you like one? You know? And if you want one, that's great. Go get one!" There's nothing wrong with having a break today. But we're not owed one.

Maybe I arrogantly do demand things from life and from people. Maybe that is part of why my relationships are bumpy and why I'm unhappy—because even when I get what I demand, I only feel like I'm getting what I should. And when I don't get it, I get real bitter and resentful and angry; because they should have given it to me.

There's no way to get in shape physically without hurting. There's no way to become like the Lord without suffering. There's no way to have a healthy marriage without pain—the pain of becoming selfless, the pain of dying to selfishness. The price tag for things that really matter is pain. And many are called, but few will do it. That's why health clubs are packed in January but empty in February. Everybody wants to get in shape, but when you start exercising, your muscles scream back at you to stop. A lot of people bail out and say, "As much as I'd like to be toned up and in shape, the price tag's too high."[1]

Part of the difficulty in dealing with pain and suffering is that we may be faced with situations that we have no control over. Most of us want control of our lives, and in our Western civilization we can do this quite well. When we no longer have control over our lives, we become vulnerable to major disappointments. We resent the situation that the event may cause. We never plan to be affected by such events.

One of the keys to getting outside our pain is to focus our attention on others. This is probably the hardest thing to do when you're in the middle of a painful experience. However, this is the starting place for healing. In helping others we heal ourselves, because our focus changes. *Psychology Today* reported an experiment involving 1700 women under stress who participated in a project to help others. Within 30 days 85 percent of the women reported that they had been relieved of their stress.

I was encouraged to do this in my own situation. By focusing on the needs of others, I began to stop feeling pity for myself. I was at a place of great discouragement because I felt I would be washed up spiritually if my marriage ended in divorce. About this time a godly mentor who would not allow me to think this way entered my life. He reminded me of David and Peter and of many others who had failed. God didn't reject them for their failures. He used the events to build them into godly men who developed willing hearts for Him.

When Moses and the people he led out of Egypt were penned between Pharaoh's troops and the Red Sea, Moses complained about the situation. God responded: "Why are you crying out to me? KEEP MOVING!" We may be in difficult circumstances in our life, but God says we are to keep moving forward!

Getting to a place in our relationship with God in which He is allowed to do anything in our lives with our full acceptance seems impossible for us. The apostle Paul reached this place: *"I know what it is to be in need, and I know what it is to have plenty. I have learned the secret of being content in any and every situation, whether well fed or hungry, whether living in plenty or in want. I can do everything through Him who gives me strength"* (Philippians 4:12-13). We must realize that God has every right to do anything He chooses to accomplish His purposes. We are not citizens of a democracy when it comes to the kingdom of God: *"I am the Lord, and there is no other. I form the light and create darkness, I bring prosperity and create disaster; I, the Lord, do all these things"* (Isaiah 45:6-7).

Job had to come to understand this firsthand. Through the first 38 chapters of Job, he expresses his turmoil over the circumstances that God had brought upon him. Finally, God hears enough and responds: *"Who is this that darkens my counsel with words without knowledge? Brace yourself like a man; I will question you, and you shall answer Me"* (Job 38:2-3).

Someone once said that when God asks a question, it's not because He doesn't know the answer. God is angry at this point. Through the next three chapters God asks Job one question after another to determine whether Job can create anything from nothing. He questions Job to the point that Job is utterly ashamed for ever bringing up the subject. For the first time Job experiences the righteous anger of God and responds:

Then Job replied to the LORD:

> *"I know that You can do all things;*
> *no plan of Yours can be thwarted.*
> *[You asked,] 'Who is this that obscures My counsel without*
> *knowledge?'*
> *Surely I spoke of things I did not understand,*
> *things too wonderful for me to know.*
> *["You said,] 'Listen now, and I will speak;*
> *I will question you,*
> *and you shall answer Me.'*
> *My ears had heard of you*
> *but now my eyes have seen You.*
> *Therefore I despise myself*
> *and repent in dust and ashes* (Job 42:2-6).

Job realizes he has seen the God of the universe Who made him and everything else and that he has absolutely no right to question anything God chooses to do. When we get to this place with God, we are never the same.

In his book, *The Three Battlegrounds*, Frances Frangipane helps us come to terms with this difficult idea:

> We weren't created to live for ourselves, but for Him. And while the Lord desires that we enjoy His gifts and His people, He would have us know we were created first for His pleasure. In these closing moments of this age, the Lord will have a people whose purpose for living is to please God with their lives. In them, God finds His own reward for creating man. They are His worshippers. They are on earth only to please God, and when He is pleased, they also are pleased. The Lord takes them farther and through more pain and conflicts than other men. Outwardly, they often seem "smitten of God and afflicted" (Isaiah 53:4). Yet to God they are His beloved. When they are crushed, like the petals of a flower, they exude a worship, the fragrance of which is so beautiful and rare that angels weep in quiet awe at their surrender. They are the Lord's purpose for creation.

One would think that God would protect them, guarding them in such a way that they would not be marred. Instead, they are marred more than other men. Indeed, the Lord seems pleased to crush them, putting them to grief. For in the midst of their physical and emotional pain, their loyalty to Christ grows pure and perfect. And in the face of persecutions, their love and worship toward God becomes all-consuming.

Would that all Christ's servants were so perfectly surren–dered. Yet God finds His pleasure in us all. But as the days of the Kingdom draw near and the warfare at the end of this age increases, those who have been created solely for worship of God will come forth in power and glory of the Son. With the high praises of God in their mouth, they will execute upon His enemies the judgment written (Psalm 149). They will lead as generals in the Lord's army of worshippers. [2]

Reflection

1. When God brings adversity into your life, what is your first response? Have you come to the place where God is allowed to bring whatever He desires in order to create Christlikeness in you?

2. What are the "entitlements" that if not received could cause you to view yourself a "victim"?

3. If God came to you today, what type of conversation might you have with Him about your own life? Would you have an attitude of grateful-ness, or would you be full of questions as to why He allowed certain things in your life?

Chapter 2

REASONS FOR ADVERSITY

I have suffered too much in this world not to hope for another.
— Jean Jacques Rousseau

There are a number of reasons why you or I will experience adversity during our lifetimes. Some segments of the church today have been wrongly taught that adversity is a sign that God has removed His blessing. Nothing could be further from the truth. The Scriptures clearly teach us that trials are a part of a walk with God. No man or woman who has achieved much in the kingdom has been spared some form of trial or adversity. God gives specific reasons for some of our trials. Other times the purpose is to identify with the cross of Christ. We must view adversity as God does—as a means to conform us to the image of His Son. Making us more Christlike is the ultimate goal of all of our experiences with God.

During this time I came across a verse of Scripture I had never noticed before. Did you know that Christ had to learn obedience? Frankly, I never thought Christ had to learn anything, much less obedience. Do you know how He learned obedience? Hebrews 5:8 says, *"Although He was a Son, He learned obedience from the things which He suffered."* Christ had to learn obedience through suffering, and He uses suffering in our lives to teach us obedience.

Therefore, since Christ suffered for us in the flesh, arm yourselves also with the same mind, for he who has suffered

in the flesh has ceased from sin, that he no longer should
live the rest of His time in the flesh for the lusts of men,
but for the will of God (1 Peter 4:1-2).

C.S. Lewis, in his book *The Problem With Pain*, wrote, "God whispers to us in our pleasures, speaks in our conscience, but shouts in our pains: it is His megaphone to rouse a deaf world." A friend described suffering as God's manure for spiritual growth. No matter what God does in our lives, we know that nothing happens without His foreknowledge and His planning. Sometimes we fall into the trap of thinking that God is not aware of our circumstances.

O LORD, you have searched me
and you know me.
You know when I sit and when I rise;
You perceive my thoughts from afar.
You discern my going out and my lying down;
You are familiar with all my ways (Psalm 139:1-3).

Peter, an apostle of Jesus Christ,
To God's elect, strangers in the world, scattered throughout
Pontus, Galatia, Cappadocia, Asia and Bithynia, who have
been chosen according to the foreknowledge of God the
Father, through the sanctifying work of the Spirit,
for obedience to Jesus Christ and sprinkling by His blood:
Grace and peace be yours in abundance (1 Peter 1:1-2).

Certain calamities simply cannot be explained adequately to allow rational defense of the events. These are better left unresolved until we come before God and He can quiet our hearts.

However, some adversity can be attributed to God's working in our lives in one of six areas: (1) sin, (2) sonship, (3) identification with others who will go through similar experiences, (4) testing, (5) preparation, and (6) experiencing God's faithfulness. He can be working in all of these areas at once or in just one or two. There are specific reasons for some of these adverse circumstances. Some of the reasons are external—events we don't cause but which deeply affect our lives. Others can be attributed to actions we take that result in pain or suffering.

Sin

We can bring adversity on ourselves through our own sin. There are countless examples of this throughout the Bible. If we have committed our lives to Jesus Christ, He is committed to loving us as a father loves his own child. When we steer away from His guiding hand, we must be brought back to obedience. Our waywardness separates us from God. God, being faithful to His character, has a responsibility to bring us back to a right relationship with Him. He must take action, for He cannot tolerate sin. He is a Holy God. When the people of Israel left the promised land they continually fell into sin. If they weren't grumbling against His provision, they were worshipping idols or some iniquity. God had to judge the people for their sin, but He never lost His love for them.

Since they hated knowledge
and did not choose to fear the LORD,
since they would not accept my advice
and spurned my rebuke,
they will eat the fruit of their ways
and be filled with the fruit of their schemes.
For the waywardness of the simple will kill them,
and the complacency of fools will destroy them (Proverbs 1:29-32).

Again the anger of the LORD burned against Israel, and He incited David against them, saying, "Go and take a census of Israel and Judah" (2 Samuel 24:1).

David was conscience-stricken after he had counted the fighting men, and he said to the LORD, "I have sinned greatly in what I have done. Now, O LORD, I beg you, take away the guilt of your servant. I have done a very foolish thing" (2 Samuel 24:10).

So the LORD sent a plague on Israel from that morning until

*the end of the time designated, and seventy thousand of the
people from Dan to Beersheba died* (2 Samuel 24:15).

But Samuel replied:
*"Does the LORD delight in burnt offerings and sacrifices as
much as in obeying the voice of the LORD?*
*To obey is better than sacrifice, and to heed is better than the
fat of rams. For rebellion is like the sin of divination, and
arrogance like the evil of idolatry. Because you have rejected
the word of the LORD, he has rejected you as king"*
(1 Samuel 15:22-23).

*But your iniquities have separated you from your God;
your sins have hidden his face from you,
so that he will not hear* (Isaiah 59:2).

*You rebuke and discipline men for their sin;
you consume their wealth like a moth—
each man is but a breath* (Psalm 39:11).

*Some became fools through their rebellious ways
and suffered affliction because of their iniquities*
(Psalm 107:17).

There are other Scriptures (too numerous to include here) that deal
with God's judgment of sin. Causes and effects of sin are described
throughout Scripture.

My father died in an airplane crash when I was 14, and our family had
to make major adjustments in our standard of living. Whenever my mother
complained about finances, I subconsciously registered a message in my
brain that I would never experience financial need again. Later, symptoms
of a stronghold of fear and insecurity showed up in the ways I related to
my wife and to the people at the office. My focus was a life message that
said I must succeed and make money.

We all have life messages. For some the message is that they are never good enough. These people often seek to prove to their parents they are successful. Others may feel they are not attractive, so they focus on achieving worldly beauty to gain acceptance. "I'm not pretty enough to be acceptable" becomes their life message. These people may undergo plastic surgery to insure their beauty. We can spend our adult lives living out these and other life messages until we realize the negative fruit that these habits ultimately bear. In most cases we are believing lies. But until someone can help us recognize these lies, we will continue to live out our particular life messages.

My anxiety-based need for financial security forced me to make decisions out of fear. It led me to accumulate, invest, and hoard. I thought I was simply being a good steward of the resources God had provided, but I discovered the truth when I saw a pattern of control impact my relationships when my finances were affected negatively. Even though this happened on a subconscious level, it was still sin—idolatry and greed stimulated by insecurity and fear. God removed my wealth in an effort to bring me back to a loving relationship with Him that would not be fear-based. I am grateful for His loving reproof that led me to discover that my security is in His care for me. One of the books that was instrumental in my coming to this understanding was a workbook by Mike and Sue Dowgiewicz called *Demolishing Strongholds*. This practical tool helped me identify these influences and their spiritual origins.

It is natural to ask, "Why does God allow us to stay in a painful situation for an extended period?" I have thought about this question often. My divorce circumstances were so painful I felt like dying at times. After almost two-and-a-half years I was still separated. Part of my pain was self-inflicted, since I refused to file for divorce. (It was a cost of obedience. The Lord showed me through this period that the errors I made in my marriage were lasting memories and consequences of these mistakes.) Some of the consequences from those mistakes remained with me. Although He doesn't want us to live in the past once we've been forgiven, the emotional pain was a reminder of the situation. God wants us to desire His best and places us in situations that will encourage us to never return to what got us into that condition in the first place. Few people who make major financial errors get out of them quickly. It seems God lets us experience the fruit of our decisions before He changes the circumstances. This is part of our spiritual growth and His reproof in our lives. Those years were also a time of learning long-suffering and patience.

Reflection

1. Can you identify a current sin for which God may be reproving you? Does your suffering relate specifically to the area of sin; i.e., financial sin leading to a financial problem, sexual sin manifesting sexual problems, attitudinal sin opening a door to family problems with a child or spouse, or rebellion of a child which could relate to a problem with authority at work? Often a sin will have a direct correlation to the adversity we face.

    Do not be deceived: God cannot be mocked. A man reaps what he sows. The one who sows to please his sinful nature, from that nature will reap destruction; the one who sows to please the Spirit, from the Spirit will reap eternal life (Galatians 6:7-8).

    If this is the case, confess your sin and seek to walk in freedom from that sin: *"If we confess our sins, He is faithful and just and will forgive us our sins and purify us from all unrighteousness"* (1 John 1:9).

2. Seek out another individual to stand with you as you confess your sins before God: *"Therefore confess your sins to each other and pray for each other so that you may be healed. The prayer of a righteous man is powerful and effective"* (James 5:16).

3. Is there any underlying bitterness toward God or toward other individuals that may be hindering you from becoming emotionally free and receiving the fullness of God's love? *"See to it that no one misses the grace of God and that no bitter root grows up to cause trouble and defile many"* (Hebrews 12:15).

Sonship

Strength is born in the deep silence of long-suffering hearts;
not amid joy.
                              —Felicia Hemans

Suffering and adversity are parts of our heritage as sons and daughters of God. They come with the territory as God's refining process for every believer. Consider every major character in the Bible, and you will see that their lives had adversity. For example, Paul's life was filled with ship-wrecks, beatings, ridicule, and even a personal malady. John the Baptist, who lived only a few short years, had his head cut off. Many of the disciples died martyr deaths for their faith. God never said we would not suffer as Christians. Throughout Scripture God encourages us not to put too much emphasis on the here-and-now life, but to emphasize our future life in heaven. Whatever trials we will encounter here will not compare to the glory He will reveal when we get to heaven. Earth is a mere watering hole on the way to eternity.

The Lord disciplines His children in order to make them more like Himself. I do not totally understand why human nature is such that adversity spurs us on to seek God more. But it surely is true in the lives of believers. If we do not share in the sufferings and discipline of Christ as His children, then we do not share in His glory:

Now if we are children, then we are heirs—heirs of God and
co-heirs with Christ, if indeed we share in His sufferings in
order that we may also share in His glory (Romans 8:17).

My son, do not despise the LORD's discipline
and do not resent His rebuke,
because the LORD disciplines those He loves,
as a father the son He delights in (Proverbs 3:11-12).

Blessed is the man You discipline, O LORD,
the man You teach from Your law (Psalm 94:12).

A fool spurns his father's discipline,
but whoever heeds correction shows prudence (Proverbs 15:5).

And you have forgotten that word of encouragement that addresses you
as sons: My son, do not make light of the Lord's discipline, and do not
lose heart when He rebukes you, because the Lord disciplines those He
loves, and He punishes everyone He accepts as a son. Endure
hardship as discipline; God is treating you as sons. For what son is not
disciplined by his father? If you are not disciplined (and everyone
undergoes discipline), then you are illegitimate children and not true
sons. Moreover, we have all had human fathers who disciplined us and
we respected them for it. How much more should we submit to the
Father of our spirits and live! Our fathers disciplined us for a little
while as they thought best; but God disciplines us for our good, that we
may share in His holiness. No discipline seems pleasant at the time, but
painful. Later on, however, it produces a harvest of righteousness and
peace for those who have been trained by it. Therefore, strengthen your
feeble arms and weak knees (Hebrews 12:5-12).

The above verses clearly describe God's role as a father who disciplines
His children. However, this discipline is not just to make us suffer; it is to
produce things in us that only this correction will produce—righteousness
and peace. He tells us that if we are removed from this discipline, then we
are really not true sons of the most holy God.

Others went out on the sea in ships;
they were merchants on the mighty waters.
They saw the works of the LORD,
His wonderful deeds in the deep.
For He spoke and stirred up a tempest
that lifted high the waves.
They mounted up to the heavens and went down to the depths;
in their peril their courage melted away.
They reeled and staggered like drunken men;
they were at their wits' end.
Then they cried out to the LORD in their trouble,
and He brought them out of their distress.

He stilled the storm to a whisper;
the waves of the sea were hushed.
They were glad when it grew calm,
and He guided them to their desired haven (Psalm 107:23-30).

Psalm 107:23-30 provides one of the best descriptions we have of God's activity in a believer's life. God describes the mighty waters we encounter at different times in our lives. The Lord Himself stirs up the tempest that lifts high the waves, but it is during these times that we see the works of God. We experience the difficult human emotions that take us to the depths of despair. The pain and suffering can make us feel drunk at times. They drive us to our wits' end; but if we cry out to the Lord, He will hear our cries and respond to us in these times. He will still the storms in His time. He will bring us through the storms and guide us to our desired havens. He allows these experiences so that we can learn that His strength is sufficient and available to us. He doesn't always deliver us from them.

R.G. LeTourneau

R.G. LeTourneau was a businessman who used business as a platform for serving God. Adversity was a major reason for his steadfast commitment to Christ. Born in 1888, LeTourneau is credited for inventing many modern-day, earth-moving machines. He was an extraordinary engineer who designed many different kinds of equipment, but it was not until after much tragedy and suffering that LeTourneau became successful. (He was not well-educated for someone who accomplished such feats.)

The following is from *More Than Conquerors*, the biography of LeTourneau:

> His relationship with Christ made an immediate difference in the way in which he approached life's challenges. Rather than fighting nose to nose with the obstacles and hardships he encountered, he instead began to look for divine purpose in each suffering or setback—and there were plenty. Shortly after his conversion, for example, the foundry where he worked burned to the ground throwing him out of work and threatening his apprenticeship.

When he moved to San Francisco to seek work there, he found himself awakened in the middle of the famous 1906 earthquake. After he finished his apprenticeship, he moved on to Stockton, California, where he began honing his skills as a mechanic and subsequently built a successful automobile dealership.

Even that period of his life was not without suffering. From having endured a broken neck in a stock-car crash, he had survived a gasoline-doused flash fire in his repair shop, he had alienated his father-in-law for seven years by marrying young seventeen-year-old Evelyn, he nearly died of Spanish influenza, lost his firstborn son at less than four months of age, and was sent into bankruptcy as a result of an inept business partner.

These hardships, more than any other factor in his development as a Christian, forged LeTourneau's spiritual priorities and submission to God. When the death of his son in 1919 brought him to the lowest point of his life, LeTourneau did not try to blame God for his misfortunes. Instead, he opened his heart, asking candidly, "Where have I gone wrong?"

It was then he believes God said to him, "My child, you have been working hard, but for the wrong things. You have been working for material things when you should have been working for spiritual things."

In LeTourneau's own account of that time in his life, he recalls: "The words were few, but the meaning ran deep. All that long night I reviewed my past, and saw where I had been paying only token tribute to God, going through the motions of acting like a Christian, but really serving myself and my conscience instead of serving Him. Instead of being a humble servant, I was taking pride in the way I was working to pay my material debts at the garage, while doing scarcely a thing to pay my spiritual debt to God.

"For my lesson that night I can now say that when a man realizes that spiritual things are worth more—and certainly they will last when material things are gone—he will work harder for spiritual things. I discovered then that God loves us

26

so much that He wants us to love Him in return. He wants us to cooperate with His program." Alluding to Matthew 6:33 regarding seeking the kingdom of God first, he added, "That I had not been doing. I had been seeking first my own way of life, and I firmly believe God had to send those difficulties into our lives to get us to look up into His face and call upon Him for His help and guidance."[4]

It was the adversity that molded the apostle Paul into the greatest warrior for Christ the world has ever known. Don't you think Paul must have thought, "Here I am doing all this for you, God; and this is how you treat me?" Paul could see the heavenly perspective to his life. Circumstances didn't matter to Paul, because he only looked through eternal lenses.

But we have this treasure in jars of clay to show that this all-surpassing power is from God and not from us. We are hard pressed on every side, but not crushed; perplexed, but not in despair; persecuted, but not abandoned; struck down, but not destroyed. We always carry around in our body the death of Jesus, so that the life of Jesus may also be revealed in our body (2 Corinthians 4:7-10).

Paul understood that life can beat us down. We can be hard pressed on every side of life, but it won't crush us. We can be confused and perplexed, but we don't have to despair. We can be persecuted, but God will not abandon us. We'll be struck down by events in life, but the events won't destroy us. We are in a continual process of dying so that Christ's life will be revealed in us.

When I was going through my adversity, there were times I wanted to leave this earth. But something inside said, "There is meaning to the trials that you are going through. I am not taking you through these just to watch you suffer." Two-and-a-half years later I began to see some of the purposes for the trials I was experiencing. Sometimes we are not privileged to know these.

God allows us to experience pain in situations to help us identify with God's own pain. Until I was rejected by my daughter during my marriage separation, I had never felt such pain. I had thought I had a good relationship with her, but her response to me was one of indifference. Part of this was her preteen age, part was her developing other interests, and part was due to the situation. In any case, the pain was very difficult for me. What God showed me in this was that He desires my fellowship and companionship as I desire fellowship and companionship with my daughter. When I reject that because I become too busy, or indifferent, I actually hurt the heart of God. When you become a father, you understand from a father's viewpoint. This experience helped me realize the pain our heavenly Father must feel when we reject or ignore Him.

Reflection

1. Have you been able to see your adversity as simply a part of being a child of God?

2. Have your adversities produced qualities that have made you more Christlike?

   And not only this, but we also exult in our tribulations, knowing that tribulation brings about perseverance; and perseverance, proven character; and proven character, hope; and hope does not disappoint, because the love of God has been poured out within our hearts through the Holy Spirit who was given to us (Romans 5:3-5).

3. What adjustments do you need to make in order to receive the grace that God has provided as a result of the adversity He has allowed you to experience?

4. Are you compensating for any pain or suffering by indulging in activities that reduce your level of pain but ultimately prolong the lesson that God is accomplishing in your life?

5. If you are fighting anger and bitterness toward God for your adversity, have you had a wrong view of God? Explain.

To Comfort Others

By afflictions God is spoiling us of what otherwise might have spoiled us. When He makes the world too hot for us to hold, we let it go.

—John Powell

Adversity will be used to frame our lives for the callings He has for us. These callings may be in areas that require us to experience the pain of those to whom we are called to minister. No one can identify with others as much as those who have experienced the same pain.

Praise be to the God and Father of our Lord Jesus Christ, the Father of compassion and the God of all comfort, who comforts us in all our troubles, so that we can comfort those in any trouble with the comfort we ourselves have received from God (2 Corinthians 1:3-4).

If we are distressed, it is for your comfort and salvation; if we are comforted, it is for your comfort, which produces in you patient endurance of the same sufferings we suffer (2 Corinthians 1:6).

During my separation and early stages of separation I experienced levels of rejection, pain, and suffering that I had never felt before. You may think that you can empathize with someone else's pain; but until you actually go through it yourself, you really can't fully understand. When I began to sit down with men who were experiencing difficulties in their marriages, I could identify with their pain as no happily married man could. When I encouraged men to stay in their marriages and resist divorce, I could say it with conviction; because I had stayed separated for over two and a half years without pursuing divorce. I knew the cost of remaining in that status.

I lost my father in an airplane crash when I was fourteen. It was difficult growing up without access to a father. When I meet another man who also lost his father at an early age, we immediately have a relationship that is different from others because of our common experience. I understand some of what that person has experienced. We are able to share at a level of understanding that others cannot.

If you lose a loved one to cancer, go through a painful operation, or experience any other suffering firsthand, you are automatically better prepared to relate to an individual who may be facing the same trial. God wants us to walk through such times in ways that we come out the other side stronger spiritually than when they began. Only then will we be able to bring real comfort and encouragement to others.

Reflection

1. Has God ever used you to comfort an individual who has faced a similar trial?

2. Have you sought to help others after someone helped you walk through a difficult time in your life?

3. Are you aware that God may have allowed you to have an experience so that you can help others in the future and that such situations are part of God's training for future ministry?

Testing

> It is only from the belief of the goodness and wisdom of a
> supreme being, that our calamities can be borne in the manner
> which becomes a man.
> —Henry Mackenzie

God discovers the depth of our relationship with Him through testing.
The Old Testament reveals countless examples of God testing His people
to determine if they would follow Him or the world's system. We are tested
on a regular basis to determine where our loyalty lies: *"If you falter in
times of trouble, how small is your strength"* (Proverbs 24:10).

Israel was tested many times as they journeyed for 40 years through
the wilderness. God showed His faithfulness often, but His testing of the
people revealed failure after failure to trust Him.

*Then the LORD said to Moses, "I will rain down bread from
heaven for you. The people are to go out each day and gather
enough for that day. In this way I will test them and see whether
they will follow My instructions"* (Exodus 16:4).

*Remember how the LORD your God led you all the way in the
desert these forty years, to humble you and to test you in order
to know what was in your heart, whether or not you would
keep His commands* (Exodus 16:4).

*I will use them to test Israel and see whether they will keep the
way of the LORD and walk in it as their forefathers did*
(Judges 2:22).

*I know, my God, that You test the heart and are pleased with
integrity. All these things have I given willingly and with honest
intent. And now I have seen with joy how willingly Your people
who are here have given to You* (Exodus 16:4).

Hezekiah was a faithful, God-honoring king for much of his life; but
toward the end he became proud. God wanted to find out if he would still
honor Him and recognize His blessings in his life. He failed the test when
an envoy was sent to his palace.

But when envoys were sent by the rulers of Babylon to ask Him about the miraculous sign that had occurred in the land, God left him to test him and to know everything that was in his heart (2 Chronicles 32:31).

God often spoke of His relationship to His people and of their rebellious hearts. He tested them to see what was in their hearts:

But they put God to the test
and rebelled against the Most High;
they did not keep His statutes (Psalm 78:56).

Therefore this is what the LORD Almighty says:
See, I will refine and test them,
for what else can I do
because of the sin of My people? (Jeremiah 9:7).

Job was tested when God allowed Satan to send calamity upon his life. God said Job was a righteous man. Here we see a man being sent calamity not for having done wrong, but actually for being a righteous man. It appears with our limited understanding that God is playing a game with Satan, and Job is the gameboard.

One day the angels came to present themselves before the
LORD, and Satan also came with them. The LORD said to
Satan, "Where have you come from?"
Satan answered the LORD, "From roaming through the earth
and going back and forth in it."
Then the LORD said to Satan, "Have you considered my servant
Job? There is no one on earth like him; he is blameless and
upright, a man who fears God and shuns evil."
"Does Job fear God for nothing?" Satan replied. "Have you not
put a hedge around him and his household and everything he
has? You have blessed the work of his hands, so that his flocks
and herds are spread throughout the land. But stretch out your
hand and strike everything he has, and he will surely curse you
to your face."
The LORD said to Satan, "Very well, then, everything he has is

in your hands, but on the man himself do not lay a finger."
Then Satan went out from the presence of the LORD
(Job 1:6-12).

On another day the angels came to present themselves before
the LORD, and Satan also came with them to present himself
before him. And the LORD said to Satan, "Where have you
come from?"
Satan answered the LORD, "From roaming through the earth
and going back and forth in it."
Then the LORD said to Satan, "Have you considered my servant
Job? There is no one on earth like him; he is blameless and
upright, a man who fears God and shuns evil. And he still
maintains his integrity, though you incited me against him to
ruin him without any reason."
"Skin for skin!" Satan replied. "A man will give all he has for
his own life. But stretch out Your hand and strike his flesh and
bones, and he will surely curse You to Your face."
The LORD said to Satan, "Very well, then, he is in your hands;
but you must spare his life" (Job 2:1-6).

Every Christian is tested, but testing is always designed to develop
something within us. There is a blessing on the other side if we are faithful
in that trial. Joseph was tested severely as he spent years in prison and
worked as a slave in Egypt. But God's testing of Joseph was important
preparation for what God had in store for him. Joseph was to save an
entire nation from starvation.

Blessed is the man who perseveres under trial, because when he has
stood the test, he will receive the crown of life that God has promised
to those who love Him (James 1:12).

We are all tested in different ways. God allows each of us a different
level of testing as we go through life to see if we will uphold His name and
be obedient. I wrongly sued a client one time and was made aware of my
error after the suit had been filed for several months. Through counsel I
realized my primary issue should have been with a vendor, not with the
client. Although the client was not totally blameless in the situation, I had

to make restitution for my contribution. Instead of forcing the client to own up to his role in the matter, I needed to accept full responsibility and allow God to convict him. The decision was made with great financial cost—over $140,000. I had to pay $40,000 of this for vendor costs. In this case I had to decide if I would make an outcome-based decision that might financially benefit me or an obedience-based decision that was right before God.

Reflection

1. Have you ever been misunderstood or wrongly accused in a situation over which you had no control? Describe your response. Did you respond the way Christ would have?

2. Can you see that God was allowing this to test you in your response to the situation?

3. Were you able to respond without blaming or making yourself the victim? Describe one situation where you failed to respond correctly and what you could have done differently.

4. How will you seek to respond in the future?

5. What situations are you in right now that could be tests from the Lord?

Obedience

God uses adversity and even affliction to teach us to live obedient lives. He used them in Jesus' life to teach Him obedience. God tests our obedience to His ways. At what point will we disobey His commands and follow our own ways? He asks us to do things that go against logic at times in order to find out what is in our hearts. Will we trust Him completely?

Although He was a son, He learned obedience from what He suffered (Hebrews 5:8).

We know that we have come to know Him if we obey his commands. The man who says, "I know Him," but does not do what He commands is a liar, and the truth is not in him. But if anyone obeys His word, God's love is truly made complete in him. This is how we know we are in Him: Whoever claims to live in Him must walk as Jesus did (Hebrews 5:8).

Therefore, since Christ suffered in His body, arm yourselves also with the same attitude, because he who has suffered in his body is done with sin. As a result, he does not live the rest of his earthly life for evil human desires, but rather for the will of God (1 Peter 4:1-2).

Before I was afflicted I went astray, but now I obey Your word (1 Peter 4:1).

It was good for me to be afflicted so that I might learn Your decrees (Psalm 119:71).

If you falter in times of trouble, how small is your strength (Proverbs 24:10).

My wife and I separated. As the man, I took full responsibility for the condition of my marriage. Knowing that God hates divorce and that it would be wrong for me to encourage any actions that would lead to a termination of our marriage, I did everything within my power to reconcile. I knew I was still married and that God required me to love my wife as Christ loved the church, sacrificially. Finally, my wife stated she wanted a divorce. Would I encourage getting the divorce over quickly and try to salvage my life materially? After more than two years I was still separated.

At the same time my business was failing, and my cash reserves were dwindling. God was requiring me to learn to trust Him and to wait on Him no matter the outcome. God used this time to teach me to obey His commands and to wait on Him. I learned important lessons in perseverance, trust, and obedience that only these experiences could have taught me. Like the apostle Paul I felt *"hard pressed on every side, but not crushed; perplexed, but not in despair; persecuted, but not abandoned; struck down, but not destroyed"* (2 Corinthians 4:9).

Reflection

1. When difficult times come, does your obedience to God increase or decrease? Describe a recent situation that created adversity for you. How did your response align itself with Scripture?

2. Was your response based on getting rid of the problem or on doing what you knew was right? What course of action did you follow?

3. Did others help you make key decisions in the process?

4. If your decision involved personal suffering on your part, what were your temptations?

Preparation

> I thank God for my handicaps, for through them, I have found
> myself, my work and my God.
> —Helen Keller

God uses the events and circumstances in our lives teach and prepare
us for the missions He has for us. Do we grumble like the Israelites? God
knows what He wants to do and who He can choose to carry out His plan.
Can God use us, or will we live our lives solely for our own pleasures?
Joseph, Mordecai, Esther and Lazarus are four people God took through
the fire for His greater purposes.

Joseph spent 13 years imprisoned or enslaved for deeds not deserving
such treatment. He was wrongly judged and imprisoned, but God used
these things to fulfill His plan to save a nation: *"But God sent me ahead of
you to preserve for you a remnant on earth and to save your lives by a great
deliverance. So then, it was not you who sent me here, but God. He made
me father to Pharaoh, lord of his entire household and ruler of all Egypt"*
(Genesis 45:7-8).

Joseph learned early that his life was not normal. His brothers threw
him in a pit, and he was later sold into slavery. If there were any Bible
character who had the right to ask God why, it would be Joseph. But God's
time of testing for Joseph was needed to prepare him for what he was
going to do in the future. It was a time for refining his character. Joseph
was a *type* of Christ whose life was used to save the lives of his people.
He gave up his own life (through slavery) for the sake of his own people.
It wasn't voluntary; circumstances put Joseph into this position. God gave
him a dream as a teen, but I am sure he had no idea what that dream
really meant until he became second in command to Pharaoh.

Mordecai was the cousin of Esther, whose parents died and was
brought into the court of King Xerxes. Through the favor of the king
toward Esther, the Jews were saved from annihilation at the hand of
Haman. God allowed Mordecai and Esther to save the king's life by
informing the king through Mordecai. As a result, the king later honored

Mordecai for his good deed toward him. He became second in command in an ungodly kingdom, just as Joseph had. God's omnipotent plan allowed Mordecai to gain favor by placing him in the right place at the right time in order to save the Jewish people through Esther. Mordecai helped Esther realize the position God had placed her. But she had to be willing to risk her life on behalf of her people:

> *For if you remain silent at this time, relief and deliverance for the Jews will arise from another place, but you and your father's family will perish. And who knows but that you have come to royal position for such a time as this?* (Esther 4:14).

> *Mordecai the Jew was second in rank to King Xerxes, preeminent among the Jews, and held in high esteem by his many fellow Jews, because he worked for the good of his people and spoke up for the welfare of all the Jews* (Esther 10:3).

Mordecai was a servant who worked for the good of the people. God knew He could use Mordecai and Esther at this time in history to save their people. Both Esther and Mordecai had to become willing to die for the cause before God would intervene in their situation.

Lazarus was allowed to die because God had a greater purpose and preparation He was accomplishing. Jesus' seeming lack of response to Mary and Martha's request to come quickly resulted in Mary and Martha feeling Jesus had let them down. But Jesus knew this delay was necessary. Their pain would be only for a little while. Jesus allowed Lazarus to remain in the grave for four days in order to demonstrate a miracle that would be a primary reason for the large turnout when Jesus rode into Jerusalem on a donkey.

> *When He heard this, Jesus said, "This sickness will not end in death. No, it is for God's glory so that God's Son may be glorified through it." Jesus loved Martha and her sister and Lazarus* (John 11:4-5).

> *Now the crowd that was with Him when He called Lazarus from the tomb and raised him from the dead continued to spread*

*the word. Many people, because they had heard that He had
given this miraculous sign, went out to meet Him. So the
Pharisees said to one another, "See, this is getting us nowhere.
Look how the whole world has gone after Him"* (John 12:17-19).

*For it is God who works in you to will and to act according to
His good purpose* (Philippians 2:13).

*And we know that in all things God works for the good of those who love
Him, who have been called according to His purpose* (Romans 8:28).

In my own life I see how God has been preparing me to be more
useful to others. I have made enough mistakes and have had enough life
experiences for me to be useful in the lives of others. I can also see that
God has used, and is still using, my trials to bring me to death in myself
so that I will seek Christ alone and His sufficiency. My trials have helped
me detach from the world and focus on what is important.

Our lives are framed by the events and experiences we are allowed to face
in life. A mature man of God once said to me, "You are a blessed man. God
does not allow a man to be tested as you have been unless He has a special
purpose planned for you." (The man who spoke these words had gone
through the fires of testing and purification himself.) We will all face different
levels of testing depending on the calls God has for our lives. After two years
of being in this fire, I began to see some of God's plans in my life and to
understand why it was necessary for me to go through what I had as
preparation for what He was calling me into. I am grateful for the glimpses
He reveals from time to time. Some people never see them.

The Desert Places

*"Therefore I am now going to allure her;
I will lead her into the desert
and speak tenderly to her.
There I will give her back her vineyards,
and will make the Valley of Achor a door of hope.
There she will sing as in the days of her youth,
as in the day she came up out of Egypt.*

"In that day," declares the LORD,
"you will call Me 'my husband';
you will no longer call Me 'my master.'
I will remove the names of the Baals from her lips;
no longer will their names be invoked" (Hosea 2:14-17).

God shows us in the story of Hosea that He purposely takes His people into the desert to prepare them and teach them. In verse 14 God talks about Gomer—a prostitute who represents the nation of Israel. He says He doesn't intend to destroy her. She will even get her vineyards back, and the Valley of Achor (which means "trouble") will actually be her door of hope. Would you ever consider trouble a door of hope? He goes on to explain that she will sing again as she had done as a child. For a person to be able to sing in the desert, some type of transformation has to take place. He explains that transformation in verse 16—she will no longer be a slave but a wife. What is the difference? The slave has been in bondage. When she becomes a bride, the Baals will no longer be in her life.

Sometimes God has to take us into the wilderness so that we will listen to Him and so that He can remove the Baals (idols) of our lives. Clearly this is what God did in my life. He pulled me aside for over two and a half years into a dessert experience to remove that which He did not want in my life. I had to make attitude adjustments along the way in order to experience His grace during those times in which I no longer wanted to remain in the desert. This time was to prepare me for a whole new calling He had planned. While I was on this journey, God brought many people into my life who had had similar desert experiences, especially in the business arena. This was the marketplace God was calling me to.

To Experience God's Faithfulness

Affliction comes to us, not to make us sad but sober; not to
make us sorry but wise.
                    —Henry Ward Beecher

If we cannot trust God in the tough times, when can we trust Him?
Through adversity we learn that we can trust Him even in the most
difficult times. Until we are tested, we really do not know how committed
we are to what we believe. Difficulties disclose how we're doing and how
we will respond to life's trials. When my wife and I had our most difficult
times, I made a statement like the following: "If you hadn't done that,
I never would have said that." I was saying that I could blame her for
my behavior. I love the following quote which says a lot about what
difficulties reveal in us:

The circumstances of life,
The events of life,
And the people around me in life,
Do not make me the way I am,
But reveal the way I am.
                    —Sam Peeples

We must all experience grace to know that it really exists, and the only
way to experience grace is to have to rely upon it. Trials are the best way
to experience His grace to the level that it is not our own strength.

*Let us then approach the throne of grace with confidence, so
that we may receive mercy and find grace to help us in our time
of need* (Hebrews 4:16).

*The LORD is close to the brokenhearted
and saves those who are crushed in spirit* (Psalm 34:18).

*He heals the brokenhearted
and binds up their wounds* (Psalm 147:3).

*And my God will meet all your needs according to His glorious
riches in Christ Jesus* (Philippians 4:19).

He has delivered us from such a deadly peril, and He will
deliver us. On Him we have set our hope that He will continue
to deliver us (2 Corinthians 1:10).

When all of the events listed in Chapter 1 occurred in my life in such a short time span, I wondered if I was going to be able to make it through without having a nervous breakdown. When you've built your life around family, business, and finances and your world falls apart quickly, you find out what you're really made of. I could handle only so much before God allowed me to be totally broken. Then I experienced God's faithfulness to carry me through this time, as He led me into relationships with key people who would help me bear the load. At one point He gave me a Scripture regarding my situation. I knew He was speaking to me through these verses:

> *Although the Lord gives you the bread of adversity and the*
> *water of affliction, your teachers will be hidden no more; with*
> *your own eyes you will see them. Whether you turn to the right*
> *or to the left, your ears will hear a voice behind you,*
> *saying, "This is the way; walk in it." Then you will defile your*
> *idols overlaid with silver and your images covered with gold;*
> *you will throw them away like a menstrual cloth and say to*
> *them, "Away with you!"*
> *He will also send you rain for the seed you sow in the ground, and*
> *the food that comes from the land will be rich and plentiful. In that*
> *day your cattle will graze in broad meadows* (Isaiah 30:20-23).

This passage spoke directly to situations I was facing. If we cannot experience the faithfulness of God in the difficult times, chances are slim we will experience His faithfulness at all. I have read stories of many who have experienced pain and suffering. Without exception, those who sought God in their storm experienced Him on a new level that they would not trade for anything else. In all cases they cited they would go through the pain again to experience this new level of relationship with God.

One time when the disciples were out on the sea, a storm arose. Jesus had not started the trip with them but came to them on the water in the midst of the storm. When the disciples looked out on the water, they screamed, "It's a ghost!" What they thought was a ghost was actually Jesus. So often what we think is something terrible when we first encounter it, turns out to be something altogether different. This situation turned out to be an opportunity for Peter to walk on water and to learn an important faith lesson—that every time we put our eyes on the circumstances, we will fail. Peter sank when he looked at the situation as he understood it. When he kept his eyes on Jesus, he succeeded. This was preparation for Peter and the rest of the disciples. I think Jesus would have been pleased if every one of the disciples had gotten out of the boat and come to him. Peter, the real winner here, was the only one who had the faith to step out of the boat. Are we willing to experience failure if our faith will grow as a result?

If you are facing a trial right now, realize that God is aware of the situation and that He has things in motion. Scripture teaches us that the negative events are being worked out for good if we love Him and are seeking to honor Him in spite of the circumstance. He will reveal His faithfulness through the situation if you will allow Him to do so.

For it is God who works in you to will and to act according to His good purpose (Philippians 2:13).

And we know that in all things God works for the good of those who love Him, who have been called according to His purpose (Romans 8:28).

Reflection

1. What would be an act of faith for you right now in your situation?

2. Are you seeking to love God so that He can make all things work for your good? If not, what things need to be changed?

3. Commit yourself to the purposes that God has in your adversity. His grace will be revealed as you trust Him.

4. Know that the pain you may be experiencing will not last forever. It is a season God is taking you through.

Chapter 3

SICKNESS AND SUFFERING

Affliction, like the iron-smith, shapes as it smites.
—Christian Nestell Bovee

Sickness in the Bible can be traced to four main sources:

1. God allows sickness to bring glory to Himself and to teach His children more about Him.

2. He allows it as judgment on sin.

3. It is sometimes an affliction from Satan.

4. He uses it to bring our earthly time on earth to an end.

Sickness and evil sometimes make it difficult for us to view God as a loving God. One psalmist said that sickness had a specific role to play in his life: *"It was good for me to be afflicted so that I might learn your decrees"* (Psalm 119:71). He saw sickness as a tool to learn God's Word.

It is also clear that God used sickness throughout the Bible to bring judgment on sin. On other occasions it was used by Satan with God's permission, i.e., in Job's life. Finally, none of us will live forever; and sickness may eventually enter our bodies to bring our lives to a close.

Lazarus

Lazarus was allowed to die because God had a greater purpose and preparation to accomplish. His actions were very painful to Mary and Martha. But He knew they were necessary. Their pain would be only for a little while.

> *When He heard this, Jesus said, "This sickness will not end in death. No, it is for God's glory so that God's Son may be glorified through it." Jesus loved Martha and her sister and Lazarus* (John 11:4-5).

> *Now the crowd that was with Him when he called Lazarus from the tomb and raised him from the dead continued to spread the word. Many people, because they had heard that He had given this miraculous sign, went out to meet Him. So the Pharisees said to one another, "See, this is getting us nowhere. Look how the whole world has gone after Him"* (John 12:17-19).

Jesus allowed Lazarus to lie dead for four days in order to demonstrate a tremendous miracle that would be the primary reason for the large turnout when He rode into Jerusalem on a donkey. He also wanted to teach Mary and Martha about trust.

My good friends Sally and Bob were going through a difficult time. Bob had been in the hospital several times within a few months and was in the hospital again. Sally could not understand why he was suffering again with those illnesses. Did Bob have sin in his life? What was the reason for this illness? Why was he not getting any better? I was not aware of Sally's struggle with these questions the Saturday morning I began my Bible-study time and was reading John 9:1-3:

> *And as He passed by, He saw a man blind from birth. And His disciples asked Him, saying, "Rabbi, who sinned, this man or his parents, that he should be born blind?" Jesus answered, "It was neither that this man sinned nor his parents; but it was in order that the works of God might be displayed in him"*

An inner voice prompted me to think of Sally as I read this passage; and as I continued in my devotional time, she kept coming to mind. Finally, I concluded that I was to share these verses with Sally and called her. She was not in, so I left a message about the passage I had been reading. I did not know what it might mean for her. That night Sally called me and said those words were indeed meant for her. That morning at the hospital she had asked her husband if he had any sin that might have resulted in this illness. Then, a Christian doctor had said to Sally that he thought this illness was meant for God's glory and that the Lord wanted Sally to know that her concerns could be put aside. God had used two of His servants to convey the message to her. (This story has a positive ending. Sally's husband was healed of his illness).

Joni Earekson Tada was like any other teenager until she dived off a lake dock. Paralyzed from the neck down, she sought God's healing for many years to no avail. As she learned to accept the condition, God used this life-changing handicap to minister His grace to hundreds of thousands of other handicapped people. Her courage and faith have inspired many. Joni has learned to paint with her mouth, to sing, and to write. Also, she has a regular radio program and an international ministry that reach out to handicapped and non-handicapped alike.

Illness Due to Sin

Paul tells us that some sickness can be traced to sin. Before believers in the early church took communion, they were to make sure they had no unconfessed sin. Paul cites that many were taking communion without having confessed. He tells the Corinthians that there is a direct relationship between illnesses and deaths in their church and their failure to take communion righteously. Does this principle still hold true today? Most definitely. It is difficult to draw direct connections; but when people become sick, it is possible that the illnesses could be a result of their continued walking with unconfessed sin while maintaining images of righteousness. This leads them to defile the communion cup.

Therefore, whoever eats the bread or drinks the cup of the Lord in an unworthy manner will be guilty of sinning against the

body and blood of the Lord. A man ought to examine himself
before he eats of the bread and drinks of the cup. For anyone
who eats and drinks without recognizing the body of the Lord
eats and drinks judgment on himself. That is why many among
you are weak and sick, and a number of you have fallen asleep.
But if we judged ourselves, we would not come under judgment.
When we are judged by the Lord, we are being disciplined so
that we will not be condemned with the world
(1 Corinthians 11:27-32).

One of my mentors who ran a Christian retreat center tells how the
Lord awoke him early one morning to write a letter to a pastor he did not
know personally. The letter said that if the pastor did not repent of his sin
he would die. My mentor did not know what this sin was, only that the
Holy Spirit was revealing to him that there was sin. My mentor shared the
letter with a pastor who knew the man the letter was addressed to. This
pastor asked if he could sign the letter too. He showed it to another pastor
who also asked to sign it. Every pastor who read the letter asked to add
his name. Finally, another pastor who looked at the letter asked if he could
mail it; and the letter was sent. Unfortunately the man did not repent of
the sin. He contracted cancer and died within three months.
(This is a true story.)

James indicates that there can be a relationship between sin and sickness: *"And the prayer offered in faith will make the sick person well; the*
Lord will raise him up. If he has sinned, he will be forgiven" (James 5:15).

Some sickness is sent from Satan. Satan appeared before God and
asked permission to afflict Job, and God allowed him to do so in order
for Job to be tested.

Reflection

1. If you are suffering from an illness, review your situation to determine if a sin might be the cause. If there is no sin, God may have a purpose He is yet to reveal. The important thing is to realize that all things work together for good for those who love God and are called according to His purpose

2. Are you able to praise God for the illness and thank Him that He will use it for His purposes?

3. Many people have found their illnesses allowed Christ to be reflected in their lives. Could He be using your illness for greater purposes that you cannot see at this time?

Chapter 4

THREE STAGES OF RESPONSE TO ADVERSITY

Anger

When I began to experience these crises in my life, I went through three distinct stages in my relationship with God. First, I had anger. I said, "Why me, Lord?" I experienced bitterness and resentment, and I wanted to blame others and God for my trials. "You don't love me, Lord" was a common thought. I viewed myself as the victim and had many pity parties. Like many other Christians, I felt I was entitled to life, health, wealth, and happiness. Often anger is our first response. We want to blame God or others for the conditions we're in. We can easily become bitter toward God. We see ourselves as victims and feel sorry for ourselves. We may try to compensate for the pain in our lives through greed or excesses in sex, alcohol, anger, TV, shopping, or even sports.

Suck-It-Up

I experienced a second stage of reaction to my circumstances. We tough guys sometimes stick it out and get through a trial by crawling into shells and isolating ourselves. In doing this we don't get to a place with God where we believe He loves us and that our experiences are designed to do something in us for the kingdom of God. We have a suck-it-up, this-will-be-over-soon mentality. We can survive these experiences but never receive what God planned for us in going through such experiences. We put on tough exteriors and just try to gut it out and keep similar situations from happening in the future. This is not how God wants us to respond. His desire is that we look to Him, come to know Him in a more intimate way and learn from the experiences.

Acceptance With Joy

The last stage is the stage where God wants us to be. We rest in His love and accept anything that He deems necessary for the continued development of Christlikeness in us and in others He would have us minister to. I call this stage Acceptance With Joy. When we can walk through our trials and truly thank the Lord for what He is accomplishing through the difficulties, we can have an inner joy—*"The joy of the Lord is my strength"* (Nehemiah 8:10).

Paul said in Romans 8:28: *"And we know that in all things God works for the good of those who love him, who have been called according to His purpose."* Paul knew that suffering was part of becoming like Christ: *"I want to know Christ and the power of His resurrection and the fellowship of sharing in His sufferings, becoming like Him in His death, and so, somehow, to attain to the resurrection from the dead"* (Philippians 3:10-11).

It took me two years to come to the place of Acceptance With Joy in my circumstances. It took that long for me to walk through the process of becoming dead to many of the things God wanted me to let go of. I could not get to this place by self-will. It was something the Holy Spirit had to do in me. I tell people, "Continue walking and seeking God in your pain. God will meet you. But you'll never gain victory if you have any bitterness against God or other people." I am truly grateful to God for allowing me to experience those years. The pain was worth the new relationship I have with Him as a result of the experiences. I am now able to cope with events that come into my life with greater faith and acceptance.

The prophet Habakkuk knew that with the invasion by the Babylonians would change life for the worse for him and his people. His faith in God was greater than the circumstances he might have to live in:

> *Though the fig tree does not bud*
> *and there are no grapes on the vines,*
> *though the olive crop fails*
> *and the fields produce no food,*
> *though there are no sheep in the pen*

and no cattle in the stalls,
yet I will rejoice in the LORD,
I will be joyful in God my Savior.
The Sovereign LORD is my strength;
He makes my feet like the feet of a deer,
He enables me to go on the heights (Habakkuk 3:17-19).

Habakkuk says he will be joyful. He won't just suck it up and survive; he will be joyful! He will rejoice in God his Savior, knowing that whatever happens God will provide His strength to go on. God will enable him to scale greater heights. When God allows us to go through tough situations, He is also the one Who enables us to walk through them victoriously.

Reflection

1. If you are going through a difficult time in your life, what stage do you think you are in?

2. If you are in either of the first two stages, what steps do you think you will need to take to allow you to move to a place of Acceptance With Joy with God?

3. Has this experience given you a more "eternal" perspective on life versus a temporal view?

4. What things have changed in your own view of life as a result of the experience? Are you free of bitterness? If not, seek God now to help you become free of bitterness or resentment for your adversity. Write down ten things that you have learned from your adversity.

Chapter 5

HOLINESS THROUGH SUFFERING

It requires more courage to suffer than to die.
—Napoleon Bonaparte

God's purpose in this process of suffering is to bring about holiness in us. He wants to produce righteousness, for without holiness we can't see God. There are souls out there that are dependent on you and me to become usable by God. As long as we have wills of our own, this process cannot happen. Jesus knew that suffering produced obedience and that obedience was necessary for every believer to fulfill what God wanted for his life (see Hebrews 5:8).

Paul says that tribulations are designed to give us hope. The path begins with tribulations, which produce perseverance, which produces character, which then produces hope. There is a progression from one step to the next.

And not only this, but we also exult in our tribulations, knowing that tribulation brings about perseverance; and perseverance, proven character; and proven character, hope; and hope does not disappoint, because the love of God has been poured out within our hearts through the Holy Spirit who was given to us (Romans 5:3-5).

Consider it pure joy, my brothers, whenever you face trials of many kinds, because you know that the testing of your faith develops perseverance. Perseverance must finish its work so that you may be mature and complete, not lacking anything (James 1:2-4).

Jacob lost all hope when his sons returned from Egypt and told him that Simeon was unable to return to him with the rest of his sons. Joseph had prevented the brothers from taking him to insure that he (Joseph) could see Benjamin—the youngest son. In Jacob's view, he had lost Joseph and Simeon, and now he could lose Benjamin. His response was to be expected: *"Their father Jacob said to them, 'You have deprived me of my children. Joseph is no more and Simeon is no more, and now you want to take Benjamin. Everything is against me'"* (Genesis 42:36).

How often I felt during my difficult times that "everything was against me." In Jacob's situation, God had gone before Jacob and was carrying out a plan that was bigger than Jacob's understanding. He was using these painful situations to save a nation. What appeared to be the loss of three sons was actually the preservation of not only three sons but also an entire nation through his children. God asked both Abraham and Jacob to trust Him with their children.

Abraham was asked by God to sacrifice his son Isaac. After Sarah had miraculously conceived and borne Isaac in her old age, why would God ask him to do such a thing? Abraham must have agonized over how he was going to explain the disappearance, or murder, of Isaac. God wants to know if we are willing to obey Him and at what cost? Abraham believed that God would raise up a sacrifice even if it meant raising Isaac from the dead.

My twelve-year-old daughter was estranged from me for about six weeks when my wife and I were were experiencing difficulties during our separation. I did not know or understand the purposes of this painful experience; but I had to trust that God, in His all-knowing love and mercy, would make them known to me in His time.

One day under the weight of my circumstances, I reached bottom emotionally. Two dear friends confronted me lovingly: "You have indeed accepted these things as from God, but there is no joy in the fact that God is free to do these things in your life. You are a survivalist. You can handle just about anything that comes your way. But unless you believe that God has a right and privilege to do these things and unless you accept them with joy, you will return to the way you were before He brought these things into your life." These were strong words. I had not come to the place in my life where hope was the overwhelming fruit from these trials. I had experienced the tribulations; I was persevering; character was being produced in my life; but there was no overwhelming evidence of hope. I was operating with a "suck-it-up, this-will-be-over-soon" attitude versus one of "Lord, thank you for allowing these experiences; and thank You that you are accomplishing Your purposes in my life." My friends continued: "You have not yet come to the place where God is free to do anything He wants in your life. You still feel that you are entitled to certain things. You have a problem with God being God."

In the early church believers understood that God had the right to do anything He wanted. They counted it a privilege to suffer for His name. This is why Paul and Silas could sing in prison: *"But about midnight, Paul and Silas were praying and singing hymns of praise to God, and the prisoners were listening to them"* (Acts 16:25). They had the kind of relationship with God that gave them such an awareness of God's presence that circumstances really did not matter. As long as they practiced the presence of God, no circumstance could change their attitude. The next few verses describe an earthquake which shook the foundations of the prison and made the cells and doors open. God created a miracle. When we trust in God and don't grumble, He causes miracles.

But an interesting thing happened. Instead of escaping through the open doors, Paul and Silas stayed in the prison. You see, they knew that if they escaped, the guard would lose his life. It appears that Paul and Silas realized that this man needed salvation. They set aside their own needs and stayed in the prison after the earthquake. The guard, shaken that the men did not flee, asked, "What must I do to be saved?" Paul and Silas did not have to "sell" this man on salvation. They simply had to respond to the hunger that was created by the demonstration of love and the miracle of God that took place in that prison. When we look beyond our own needs, God does miraculous things.

It is one thing to walk through trials and adversity. It is an altogether different matter to walk through them with joy and thanksgiving. I had not been able to get to this place in my life. I wanted to be there. But how could I get to this place? I could not manufacture joy. This was something God had to do.

I realized that I was a product of American Christianity. I was seeking a God that I WANTED versus the God that IS. The God that I wanted was a God who would respond immediately to my cries for help and who would deliver me from pain and suffering when I prayed. But the God who IS is a God who said that Christians will suffer in this life and that adversity comes with the territory. He is the God who said Christ learned obedience through suffering (see Hebrews 5:8). This concept is difficult to accept in our follow-these-steps-and-it-will-be-okay culture. We want God to follow a prescribed formula—if we do this, He will do that. The truth is we cannot manipulate God to our own devices.

Some of us will endure greater hardships and suffering than others. Does this mean God loves one more than another? No. It simply means that God is God, and His plans are altogether different than ours; and He has the right to make such decisions because He Is God. This is difficult for Americans to swallow. Because God operates like a ruling monarchy, not like a democratic system.

Hannah Hurnard's best-selling allegory, *Hinds' Feet On High Places*, was particularly helpful to me. The author chronicles the journey of the main character, Much-Afraid, who has been called by the Shepherd to scale the mountain of Love. Her companions on the long, difficult journey are Sorrow and Suffering. Much-Afraid's relatives—Craven Fear, Aunt Dismal Forebodings, Spiteful, Gloomy, Lord Fearing, Pride, Bitterness and Resentment, and Self-Pity—do not want her to leave. In fact, they desperately want Much-Afraid to stay and comfort them. However, the Shepherd tells Much-Afraid she will not be able to keep company with these relatives if she is to climb the mountain of Love successfully.

At one point the similarities between the story and what I was experiencing in my own journey were uncanny.

Seeing the precipice she must scale:

> Much-Afraid covered her face with her hands and sank down on a
> rock with a horror and dread in her heart such as she had never felt
> before. Then she felt her two companions take her hands in theirs and
> heard them say, "Do not be afraid, Much-Afraid, this is not a dead-end
> after all, and we shall not have to turn back. There is a way up the
> face of the precipice. The hart and the hind have shown it to us quite
> plainly. We shall be able to follow it too and make the ascent."
>
> "Oh, no! No!" Much-Afraid almost shrieked. "That path is utterly
> impossible. The deer may be able to manage it, but no mere human
> being could." [5]

As I read these words, I knew that my friends Mike and Sue were my
hart and hind showing me the path to the ascent God was asking of me.
Mike kept reminding me of God's call on my life. To walk through these
trials without a positive end in sight seemed impossible. Just as it seemed
something positive was on the horizon, another event would occur to
send me back down the mountain. The most recent one was the rejection
of me by my daughter. Mike and Sue often "held my hand" when the path
was going to be particularly difficult. Father's Day was one of those times.
They anticipated this would be a difficult day for me. (It was. I never
heard from my wife or daughter that day.) Without any prompting they
bore my burden, too, simply by walking through it with me. They often
could see ahead to the mountain to be scaled and were willing to go ahead
and clear the path so that it was easier to climb.

I had to give up my "right" to my daughter at this time and trust that
despite my pain and the negative appearance of the situation all would
work for the good. If Isaac could be raised from the dead as Abraham
believed, so too, God could restore my relationship with my daughter.
(He did so later on a limited basis.)

> *And we know that in all things God works for the good of those
> who love him, who have been called according to His purpose*
> (Romans 8:28).

I also had to remember that God was going to complete the work that He intended these things to accomplish: *"Being confident of this, that He who began a good work in you will carry it on to completion until the day of Christ Jesus"* (Philippians 1:6). *"For it is God who works in you to will and to act according to His good purpose"* (Philippians 2:13).

When Much-Afraid at last reached the top of the mountain, the Shepherd gave her a new name—Grace and Glory—and her feet were transformed to hinds' feet. (*"The Lord is my strength, and he will make my feet like hinds' feet, and he will make me walk upon mine high places"* [Habakkuk 3:19].) Then the Shepherd asked her what she had learned along the way, and she recounted five important lessons.

"First," said she, "I learned that I must accept with joy all that you allowed to happen to me on the way and everything to which the path led me! That I was never to try to evade it but to accept it and lay down my own will on the altar and say, 'Behold me, I am thy little handmaiden Acceptance-With-Joy.'

"Then I learned that I must bear all that others were allowed to do against me and to forgive with no trace of bitterness and to say to thee, 'Behold me—I am thy little handmaiden Bearing-With-Love,' that I may receive power to bring good out of this evil.

"The third thing that I learned was that you, my Lord, never regarded me as I actually was, lame and weak and crooked and cowardly. You saw me as I would be when you had done what you promised and had brought me to the High Places, when it could be truly said, 'There is none that walks with such a queenly ease, nor with such grace, as she.' You always treated me with the same love and graciousness as though I were a queen already . . . My Lord, I cannot tell you how greatly I want to regard others in the same way.

"The fourth thing," said she with a radiant face, "was really the first I learned up here. Every circumstance in life, no matter how crooked and distorted and ugly it appears to be, if it is reacted to in love and forgiveness and obedience to your will can be transformed.

"Therefore I begin to think, my Lord, you purposely allow us to be brought into contact with the bad and evil things that you want changed. Perhaps that is the very reason why we are here in this world, where sin and sorrow and suffering and evil abound, so that we may let you teach us so to react to them, that out of them we can create lovely qualities to live forever. That is the only really satisfactory way of dealing with evil, not simply binding it so that it cannot work harm, but whenever possible overcoming it with good."

At last he spoke. "You have learned well, Grace and Glory. Now I will add one thing more. It was these lessons which you have learned which enabled me to change you from limping, crippled Much-Afraid into Grace and Glory with the hinds' feet. Now you are able to run, leaping on the mountains and able to follow me where I go, so that we need never be parted again.

"So remember this; as long as you are willing to be Acceptance-with-Joy and Bearing-in-Love, you can never again become crippled, and you will be able to go wherever I lead you. You will be able to go down into the Valley of the world to work with me there, for that is where the evil and sorrowful and ugly things are which need to be overcome.

"Accept and bear and obey the Law of Love, and nothing will be able to cripple your hinds' feet or to separate you from me. This is the secret of the High Places, Grace and Glory, it is the lovely and perfect law of the whole universe. It is this that makes the radiant joy of the Heavenly Places." Then he rose to his feet, drew her up beside him, and said, "Now use your hinds' feet again, for I am going to lead you to another part of the mountain."[6]

The next week while traveling on a plane, I found the words from another book jumped off the page at me, because of what I had been experiencing and reading the days before:

"Precious in the sight of the Lord is the death [death to self] of His godly ones" (Psalm 116:15, emphasis added). "The worker, who was still looking at me, then said, 'You have not died yet, but

were changed just by being close to those who have. When you die you will see even more glory.'"

Mike and Sue were those close to me who modeled death-to-self. Several weeks before I had been asked by one of my business advisory council members if I had become dead yet. When we become dead to a thing or to self-desire, it doesn't matter what happens to us. A dead man can't get offended. A dead man has no self-will. A dead man can't stand up for his own rights. A dead man can't yell or argue. A dead man has no stress. When we become dead to our own needs and wants, God can do the work He wants in us to provide those things He knows we need. When our will is truly His will, we start to see God work in our lives. This is the place every servant of God must come to in order to be used mightily in the kingdom of God. I realized this whole process had a goal of bringing me to that death place where I wanted nothing other than Jesus.

Then Jesus said to His disciples, "If anyone would come after Me, he must deny himself and take up his cross and follow Me. For whoever wants to save his life will lose it, but whoever loses his life for Me will find it" (Matthew 16:24-25).

One day as a close friend and I were talking about the events of the past months in my life, he said, "I don't understand why you are having to go through this. I've never known anyone who has gone through so much as you. I just can't see the positives in what you're going through." It took me a while before I could answer him.

I responded in this way: First, I believe that God allowed me to experience financial losses as a reproof from Him. Because of strongholds of insecurity and fear, I had allowed money to become an idol and a source of security in my life. God, in His love and concern for me as His child, had to correct me and allowed those losses so that I would return to Him as my first love and would trust Him in the financial area.

Dr. Charles Stanley in his book *Adversity* said, "God is not about to let up on a believer until He has accomplished what He has set out to do. If a man or woman refuses to give in, God will just turn up the heat. Remember, His ultimate goal for you and me is not ease, comfort, or pleasure. It is conformity to the image of His son. And He is willing to go to great lengths to accomplish His purpose. The writer of Hebrews summed it up well when he wrote,

> *All discipline for the moment seems not to be joyful, but sorrowful; yet to those who have been trained by it, afterwards it yields the peaceful fruit of righteousness* (Hebrews 12:11).[7]

Second, God is a very complex, strategic thinker. He can accomplish a lot of things with one or two events. I believe that He decided it was His will for me to go through these things to prepare me for ministry to others. What I was going through was going to be used to comfort others. God doesn't take us through difficulties just for pain's sake. It is part of His framing of our lives for His purposes (see 2 Corinthians 1:3-4,6).

Third, I can now see it was preparation for the calling He has for me in relation to business people. Men experiencing difficulties in their businesses and marriages were already crossing my path. It is difficult for most men to reconcile the fact that God uses the imperfections of our mates to make us more Christlike. It is also difficult for successful businessmen not to associate success with their own hands, but God is the source of all blessings. I have been able to share these two major lessons learned through adversity with others in business.

I also believe that I am one of many around the world God is preparing within the business world for a "Joseph-type" ministry. For the most part Christian business owners have been living in Egypt among gods of greed and pleasure. Some truly reflect Christ in their businesses; however, a majority see their business as just that—theirs. I was one of them. God is raising up Christian businessmen and businesswomen who realize that God has given them their businesses to accomplish significant things in these last days. But He has had to strip many business people of their assets in order to rebuild them His way. This trend is not just in America, but throughout the world. In some cases God restores financial blessing after they commit themselves fully to His purposes. However, this should not be construed a formula for success.

For some of us it does not take much to cause us to seek God with all of our hearts. For others, it takes an awful lot of adversity before we turn to Him fully. As I said before, I was a survivalist. I could handle just about anything that came my way. My friend Mike used to say he called me often because he'd seen men who had gone through lesser events commit suicide. God knew what it would take for me to listen with sensitive, spiritual ears. If we can handle a situation in our own strength, then He does not get the glory. *"For when I am weak, then I am strong"* (2 Corinthians 12:10). Paul knew that the thorn in his flesh was put there for his benefit to keep him dependent on God.

These events bankrupted all my human emotional strengths. I could not function without complete dependence on Him. But this is where I experienced His power. From God's perspective, it is always more important that we experience His supernatural power than it is to live pain-free, adversity-free lives. We see this example countless times throughout the Old and New Testaments. As we learn to live more and more dependent on Him for the things we lack, we experience more and more contentment no matter the state we're in; and we find our circumstances no longer dictate our emotional state.

Finally, being put in so many adverse situations in such a short time I learned about the faithfulness of God. I had known God intellectually, but I was forced to experience Him on a real need basis. There is a difference between having a knowledge of God and having an experience with God. Much of the church today has a knowledge of God, but few have had an experience with God. Each time that we experience God and His faithfulness in an adverse situation, we find our faith strengthened for the next time. We can also help others because we've been through it. We'll be able to tell others that God will be faithful to them if they will trust Him. When we are placed in difficult situations, God's grace is shed more in our lives.

Let us then approach the throne of grace with confidence, so that we may receive mercy and find grace to help us in our time of need (Hebrews 4:16).

The LORD is close to the brokenhearted and saves those who are crushed in spirit (Psalm 34:18).

He heals the brokenhearted and binds up their wounds (Psalm 147:3).

Whenever God takes us through adversity, we can be sure that these events will be used to frame our lives with the message He intends to share through us. It is part of the carving process to make us glistening diamonds in a dark world.

Reflection

1. Can you see God's purpose in your situation? If not, ask a close friend to pray that God would reveal it to you.

2. Which of the six reasons for adversity apply to your situation?

3. Have you allowed God's grace to sustain you through this time, or are you compensating for the pain in some other way?

4. Don't be afraid to walk head-on through the pain. Do not avoid facing your adversity.

Chapter 6

PEACE. A WEAPON AGAINST SATAN.

Our peace does not come from extreme indifference, nor is
it from becoming so "spiritual" that you fail to notice a
problem. It is being so confident in God's love that you
know, regardless of the battle and the difficulties in your
circumstances, that "greater is He who is in you than He
who is in the world" (see 1 John 4:4). You are not
self-assured, you are God-assured.
                    —Francis Frangipane

Webster's defines the word *peace* as "freedom from anxiety, annoyance, or
other mental disturbance: peace of mind. A state of tranquillity or serenity."

In his book, *The Three Battlegrounds*, Francis Frangipane describes our
defense in dealing with difficult circumstances. We are in the middle of
spiritual warfare that must be combated through God's power in us:

To wage effective spiritual warfare, we must understand spiritual
authority. Spiritual authority is not forcing your will upon another.
When you have spiritual authority, you have established God's peace
in an area that once was full of conflict and oppression. Therefore, to
truly be able to move in authority we must first have peace.

The apostle Paul taught, *"the God of peace will soon crush Satan
under your feet"* (Romans 16:20). When we maintain peace during
warfare it is a crushing death blow to satanic oppression and fear. Our
victory never comes from our emotions or our intellect. Our victory
comes by refusing to judge by what our eyes see or our ears hear, and
by trusting that what God has promised will come to pass.

We will never know Christ's victory in its fullness until we stop reacting humanly to our circumstances. When you truly have authority over something you can look at that thing without worry, fear or anxiety. Your peace is the proof of your victory. Jesus' authority over the violent storm (see Matthew 8:23-27) was the exercise and expansion of His peace over the elements. He did not fight against the storm, nor did He fear it. He faced its fury and subdued it with His authority, in perfect peace. In Pilate's court, in a world stirred to an emotional frenzy by the powers of hell, a holy tranquillity surrounded Christ's peace that was born out of His resolve to do God's will no matter what the cost. His Spirit emanated a calm that perfectly represented the peace at God's throne. In a matter of moments it was no longer Jesus who was on trial, but Satan, Pilate and the nation of Israel.

Satan's arsenal consists of such things as fear, worry, doubt, self-pity, etc. Every one of these weapons robs us of peace and leaves us troubled inside. Do you want to discern where the enemy is coming against you? In the network of your relation-ships, wherever you do not have peace, you have war. Conversely, wherever you have victory, you have peace. When Satan hurls his darts against you, the more peace you have during adversity, the more truly you are walking in Christ's victory.

Paul tells us to be *"in no way alarmed by your opponents— which is a sign of destruction for them, but of salvation for you"* (Philippians 1:28). Your peace, your immovable stand upon the Word of God is a sign that you are positioned correctly in perfect submission to the will of God. The very fact that you are "in no way alarmed" by your adversary is a sign that you have authority over him.

Peace is Spiritual Power. A peacemaker is not merely some-one who protests against war; he is one who is inwardly so yielded to Christ in spirit and purpose that he can be called a "son of God." Where he goes, God goes and where God goes, he goes. He is fearless, calm and bold. Peace emanates from him the way light and heat radiate fire.

In the battles of life, your peace is actually a weapon. Indeed, your confidence declares that you are not falling for the lies of the devil. You see, the first step toward having spiritual authority over the adversary is having peace in spite of our circumstances. When Jesus confronted the devil, he did not confront Satan with His emotions or in fear. Knowing that the devil was a liar, He simply refused to be influenced by any other voice than God's. His peace overwhelmed Satan, His authority then shattered the lie, which sent demons fleeing.

In the 23rd Psalm David declares, *"Yea, though I walk through the valley of the shadow of death, I will fear no evil; for Thou art with me."* There is a place of walking with God where you simply fear no evil. David faced a lion, a bear and a giant. In this psalm he stood in the "shadow of death" itself, yet he "feared no evil." David's trust was in the Lord. He said, *"...for Thou art with me."* Because God is with you, every adversity you face will unfold in victory as you maintain your faith in God! David continued, *"Thou dost prepare a table before me in the presence of my enemies."* The battle you are in will soon become a meal to you, an experience that will nourish and build you up spiritually.

Only God's peace will quell your fleshly reactions in battle. The source of God's peace is God Himself.

Peace I leave with you; My peace I give you. I do not give to you as the world gives. Do not let your hearts be troubled and do not be afraid (John 14:27).

I have told you these things, so that in Me you may have peace. In this world you will have trouble. But take heart! I have overcome the world. (John 16:33).

Before the throne there was, as it were, a sea of glass like crystal (Revelation 4:6a).

Rest precedes rule. Peace precedes power. Do not seek to

rule over the devil until you are submitting to God's rule over you. The focal point of all victory comes from seeking God until you find Him, and having found Him, allowing His Presence to fill your spirit with His peace. From full assurance at His right hand, as we rest in His victory, let us rule in the midst of our enemies."[8]

We all go through circumstances that rob our peace if we give in to the circumstances. Jesus' disciples were also faced with trying circumstances. After His death, Jesus appeared to the disciples who were fearful of the Jews.

> *On the evening of that first day of the week, when the disciples were together, with the doors locked for fear of the Jews, Jesus came and stood among them and said, "Peace be with you!" After He said this, He showed them His hands and side. The disciples were overjoyed when they saw the Lord. Again Jesus said, "Peace be with you! As the Father has sent Me, I am sending you"* (John 20:19-21).

Jesus was telling them that appropriating God's peace was the way to handle their fears. It was at this time that Jesus breathed on them the Holy Spirit. Jesus knew they could not have total peace without the power of the Holy Spirit in their lives: *"And with that he breathed on them and said, 'Receive the Holy Spirit'"* (John 20:22).

It is up to us to allow the Holy Spirit to work in our lives in such ways as to bear the fruit of the Holy Spirit in us: *"But the fruit of the Spirit is love, joy, peace, patience, kindness, goodness, faithfulness, gentleness and self-control. Against such things there is no law"* (Galatians 5:22-23).

I believe the fruit cited in this passage is a progression of our bearing each of these fruits first to bear the next. This is my personal view, as I have seen it work this way in my own life. It starts with love of God and others. As we love, we can begin to experience joy. That joy results in greater peace with God and man. Peace then yields patience, kindness, goodness, faithfulness, gentleness and self-control.

Paul tells us that in order for us to appropriate God's peace, we must do something. We must abstain from becoming anxious. We are to pray. We are to be thankful in whatever situation we find ourselves:

Do not be anxious about anything, but in everything, by prayer and petition, with thanksgiving, present your requests to God. And the peace of God, which transcends all understanding, will guard your hearts and your minds in Christ Jesus (Philippians 4:6-7).

Give thanks in all circumstances, for this is God's will for you in Christ Jesus (1 Thessalonians 5:18).

We are not actually thanking God for the negative circumstances; we are thanking Him for being God. We're thanking Him that He is still in control and that our faith is in Him, not in the circumstances. We're thankful in spite of the difficult circumstances that we face. This is where God's power is appropriated. God asks us to do a very unnatural thing— to praise Him when we're in the midst of adversity—so that He can do something supernatural in our lives—provide peace inside the circumstance.

Next, we are told we cannot experience peace unless we focus our minds and emotions on that which is true and positive. Feelings don't always accurately reflect the truth of a situation. They can be the wrong thermometer for measuring reality:

Finally, brothers, whatever is true, whatever is noble, whatever is right, whatever is pure, whatever is lovely, whatever is admirable—if anything is excellent or praiseworthy—think about such things. Whatever you have learned or received or heard from Me, or seen in Me —put it into practice. And the God of peace will be with you (Philippians 4:8-9).

Positive-thinking friends tell us it is impossible to weather a storm if we constantly look at the negative circumstances. Paul had been able to avoid letting circumstances dictate his feelings. He said, "Follow my lead." If he hadn't been able to focus on God rather than on his circumstances, he wouldn't have told them to put the same into practice. Peter had to learn this principle, too. When he jumped out of the boat to come to Jesus on the water, he began to sink as soon as he looked at the circumstances. He could have drowned! But he didn't because he was keeping his eyes on Jesus.

A victorious walk with God requires obedience. Obedience is the first step to victory over circumstances in our life. It is not enough to believe; we must also do something. When we do, God moves. When the Israelites walked around Jericho seven times in obedience to God's command, the walls fell. And it wasn't until the seventh lap that God moved. He wouldn't have acted if they had walked around only six times. The Jordan didn't begin to separate for Joshua until the priests put their toes in the water as God had directed. Faith and obedience are prerequisites to God acting.

Can peace and pain coexist in painful emotional or physical circumstances? I think they can. God would not tell us we can experience His peace in difficult circumstances if He did not also equip us to experience His peace. Jesus went through difficult circumstances, not the least of which was the cross. Yet, He had the peace of God knowing that He was doing the will of the Father, even though it was painful. In the garden at Gethsemane Jesus sweat drops of blood. Yet He had no sin. This must mean He was able to still maintain peace in the midst of inner anguish.

Jesus Appears As A Ghost

During the fourth watch of the night Jesus went out to them, walking on the lake. When the disciples saw Him walking on the lake, they were terrified. "It's a ghost," they said, and cried out in fear. But Jesus immediately said to them: "Take courage! It is I. Don't be afraid." "Lord, if it's You," Peter replied, "tell me to come to You on the water." "Come," He said. Then Peter got down out of the boat, walked on the water and came toward Jesus. But when he saw the wind, he was afraid and, beginning to sink, cried out, "Lord, save me!" Immediately Jesus reached out His hand and caught him. "You of little faith," He said, "why did you doubt?"

And when they climbed into the boat, the wind died down. Then those who were in the boat worshiped Him, saying, "Truly you are the Son of God." (Matthew 14:25-33).

When Peter and the other disciples were in the boat, they looked over the ocean and saw something that instilled fear in them. They were experienced fisherman and had been on the water many times, but this time they saw something they had never seen before. At first, it looked like a ghost. (When we first encounter things, they often instill fear in us; and we want to protect ourselves from them.) As things progressed, Peter was able to see that what he thought he saw and what was actually on the water were completely different. In fact, they were exactly opposite—it was Jesus on the water. Jesus identified Himself in the circumstance. We need to know there is no circumstance that Jesus is not in. What appears to be a very negative circumstance may indeed be something unusual, but part of something God is doing in our lives.

Peter then focused his attention on Jesus and did something miraculous—he walked on water. As long as Peter kept his eyes on Jesus, he did not sink. We can walk in peace through our circumstances through the supernatural power of Jesus. We cannot do this in our own strength. As soon as we focus on the circumstance, we lose our peace.

The leader of a men's group asked two men to stand. One was to represent Jesus, the other a circumstance. The leader said, "I want you to keep your eyes on *Jesus* and on the *circumstance* at the same time. Never take your eyes off both of them." As the two men walked away from one another, everyone in the room found it impossible to keep their eyes on both of the men. We had to look either at *Jesus* as he walked into another room or at the *circumstance*. The lesson was clear. We could not keep our eyes on both Jesus and the circumstance. We were forced to choose one or the other. Life is the same. As situations arise, our peace is dependent on what or on whom we choose to focus our attention—the circumstance, or Jesus.

Reflection

1. When an event takes place in your life that you perceive as negative, what is your first response?

2. How does your response line up with God's view of the situation?

3. What are your feelings?

4. Are your feelings based on the circumstance or on what God wants to accomplish through the situation?

5. How important was your need to understand the situation versus accepting it, knowing that God's purposes would be accomplished?

Chapter 7

AVOIDING BITTERNESS IN THE MIDST OF SUFFERING

Earth hath no sorrow that heaven cannot heal.
—Thomas Moore

"I've just about had it, God. You've taken my money and my accounts. The business is sliding. My wife is divorcing me. My vice president is running off with my accounts. Now I've lost my relationship with my only daughter!" I was angry with God! I was angry with those who were the instruments of the pain. "How much more have I got to take?" I was pretty down as I arrived at the office that day. Then the verses I read in my study time that morning disturbed me and added to my pain:

But the Lord was pleased
To crush Him, putting Him to grief;
If He would render Himself as a guilt offering,
He will see His offspring,
He will prolong His days,
And the good pleasure of the Lord will prosper in His hand.
As a result of the anguish of His soul,
He will see it and be satisfied;
By His knowledge the Righteous One,
My Servant, will justify the many,
As He will bear their iniquities.
Therefore, I will allot Him a portion with the great,
And He will divide the booty with the strong;
Because He poured out Himself to death,

And was numbered with the transgressors;
Yet He Himself bore the sin of many
And interceded for the transgressions (Isaiah 53:10-12).

For the first time I realized that God's perspective on suffering is totally different from mine. To God this suffering was needed; and because it was going to accomplish something great for others, it was good in His sight. That is very difficult to deal with. We have been duped into believing that if we follow God we will be guaranteed a painless life.

Make every effort to live in peace with all men and to be holy;
without holiness no one will see the Lord. See to it that no one
misses the grace of God and that no bitter root grows up to
cause trouble and defile many (Hebrews 12:14-15).

Here was the real issue for me. I could fight God, refuse to forgive God and others, and allow a root of bitterness to grow and cause trouble and defile many; or I could allow God to heal the hurt and do what He wanted through these events in my life. As my friend Mike often said to me, "You can go the long way or the short way." You can go around the track one more time or take the short cut. Which do you want? Boot camp is designed to get rid of a will of our own. Do you really want to be treated the way God treated His own Son? God has to break us down. He wants to get us to the place where we have no will of our own and just desire to be obedient. In the military, the commanding officers know how detrimental insubordination is to the rest of the troops. Disobedience can endanger the lives of the entire battalion. Our disobedience will affect all other believers.

When we feel we have been wronged, we have a choice to make. We can forgive those who have wronged us, or we can live in unforgiveness which leads to a stronghold of bitterness in our life. This bitterness will defile others. It is a vicious trap. Broken relationships that end in divorce of marriage partners, close friends, family members, or business relationships can be devastatingly painful experiences. The temptation to hang on to unforgiveness in order to get that person to pay for the wrong he did is overwhelming. The pain is intense, and we feel someone has to pay for that pain. We can feel justified in trying to get a "pound of flesh" for the

76

wrong inflicted. Jesus knew this kind of pain. He knew the temptation to repay with hate and unforgiveness. "Vengeance is mine; I will repay," saith the Lord" (Romans 12:19). It is not our responsibility to enforce justice.

When we refuse to forgive others, bitterness develops in us. Jesus was very firm when He taught about the need to forgive others. In fact, He said that if we refuse to forgive others, we are in jeopardy of not being forgiven ourselves:

For if you forgive men when they sin against you, your heavenly Father will also forgive you. But if you do not forgive men their sins, your Father will not forgive your sins (Matthew 6:14-15).

Then Peter came to Jesus and asked, "Lord, how many times shall I forgive my brother when he sins against me? Up to seven times?" Jesus answered, "I tell you, not seven times, but seventy-seven times" (Matthew 18:21-22).

Peter is struggling with forgiveness, and Jesus is telling Peter there is no limit to the number of times he is to forgive. As Jesus forgives us again and again, He expects us to do the same. Immediately after this answer, Jesus gives the disciples a parable to illustrate the concept of forgiveness:

Therefore, the kingdom of heaven is like a king who wanted to settle accounts with his servants. As he began the settlement, a man who owed him ten thousand talents was brought to him. Since he was not able to pay, the master ordered that he and his wife and his children and all that he had be sold to repay the debt. The servant fell on his knees before him. "Be patient with me," he begged, "and I will pay back everything." The servant's master took pity on him, canceled the debt and let him go. But when that servant went out, he found one of his fellow servants who owed him a hundred denarii. He grabbed him and began to choke him. "Pay back what you owe me!" he demanded. His fellow servant fell to his knees and begged him, "Be patient with me, and I will pay you back." But he refused. Instead, he went off and had the man thrown into prison until he could pay the debt. When the other servants saw what had happened, they were greatly distressed and went and told their master every-thing that had happened. Then the master called the servant in. "You wicked servant," he said, "I canceled all that debt of yours because you begged me to. Shouldn't you have had mercy on your fellow servant just as I had on you?" In anger his master turned him over to the jailers to be tortured, until he should pay back all he owed. This is how my heavenly Father will treat each of you unless you forgive your brother from your heart (Matthew 18:21-35).

What a picture of forgiveness! This incredible passage compares the forgiveness Christ offers to our forgiveness of others. Imagine owing someone 10,000 talents. Bible commentators estimate that 10,000 talents suggest a value of $12 million; but, with inflation and fluctuating precious metal prices, this could be over a billion dollars in today's currency. Such debts could never be repaid through slavery, which was often the way a debt was paid in Biblical times. The servant's debt is totally forgiven. In comparison, we discover that the servant is requiring the debt owed him of a hundred denarii be paid or the fellow servant be thrown in prison. This amount owed him is a few hundred dollars in terms of metal currency. It represents a hundred days' wages for a foot soldier or common laborer—a trivial amount compared to what he owed the king.

The king discovers the unforgiveness of his servant toward a fellow servant, calls him wicked (verse 32) and turns him over to the "torturers" (not merely "jailers"). The servant is to pay back all he owes, which he can never do. What a comparison Jesus is giving us of His forgiveness and our forgiveness of others. If we do not forgive others, we will be held captive to that unforgiveness. We also hold others captive when we do not release them from our bitterness.

True forgiveness is having greater concern for a person after he offends me than I did before he offended me. It is using the hurts others inflict as the basis of demonstrating Christ's love back to them. It was once said, "If someone's name is mentioned to you and you have an uneasy feeling in your heart that you'd prefer to avoid that person, chances are you are holding unforgiveness toward that person."

Unforgiveness has even been found to result in physical consequences. Ulcerative colitis, toxic goiters, and high blood pressure are only a few of the scores of diseases caused by bitterness. Our resentments call forth certain hormones from the pituitary, adrenal, thyroid and other glands. Excesses of these hormones can cause diseases in any part of the body.[9]

Refusing to forgive results in physical fatigue and loss of sleep and may even lead to other serious illnesses such as Epstein Barr or chronic fatigue syndrome. We may try to hide our resentments, but soon they will be etched into our eyes and facial muscles as permanent reflections of our inward feelings.

"The life of the flesh is in the blood" (Leviticus 17:11). But the "factory" for the blood is the marrow of our bones. The health of our bones, therefore, determines the health of our body. Bitterness has a direct and devastating effect upon our bones.[10]

Paul tells us that we are not to entertain bitterness, and he exhorts us to forgive one another. He understands that bitterness, rage and anger—even harsh words—come in the same package. Harsh words and strong emotions often accompany broken relationships. Paul admonishes us not to allow bitterness to rule:

> *Do not let any unwholesome talk come out of your mouths, but only what is helpful for building others up according to their needs, that it may benefit those who listen. And do not grieve the Holy Spirit of God, with whom you were sealed for the day of redemption. Get rid of all bitterness, rage and anger, brawling and slander, along with every form of malice. Be kind and compassionate to one another, forgiving each other, just as in Christ God forgave you* (Ephesians 4:29-32).

In the last chapter of Job, we find a key ingredient God required before He could restore Job with a family and wealth: *"After Job had prayed for his friends, the LORD made him prosperous again and gave him twice as much as he had before"* (Job 42:10). Job had three friends who wrongly judged him and who were sources of much pain for him. But

God would not restore Job until he prayed for them and forgave them. Even in this Old Testament story we see the importance God places on right relationships. Bitterness can defile many if allowed unchecked. This was a voluntary act by Job.

Peter and John encountered a man named Simon—a man of means who was impressed with what he saw when Peter and John prayed for the people who received the Holy Spirit. Peter rebuked Simon for thinking he could buy this power. After he rebuked him, he addressed the more important issue in Simon's life—bitterness. Peter cites that he could see that the man was driven by bitterness and was captive to it.

> *Then Peter and John placed their hands on them, and they received the Holy Spirit. When Simon saw that the Spirit was given at the laying on of the apostles' hands, he offered them money and said, "Give me also this ability so that everyone on whom I lay my hands may receive the Holy Spirit." Peter answered: "May your money perish with you, because you thought you could buy the gift of God with money! You have no part or share in this ministry, because your heart is not right before God. Repent of this wickedness and pray to the Lord. Perhaps he will forgive you for having such a thought in your heart. For I see that you are full of bitterness and captive to sin."* (Acts 8:17-23).

There is probably no greater problem in the body of Christ today than bitterness. Split churches, failed marriages, business breakups, parent-child breaks—the list of relationships that end in bitterness is long. Bitterness imprisons both those who keep it and those who are the recipients. We are warned against allowing a root of bitterness to grow (see Hebrews 12:14-15), because the damage that bitterness can do to many is tremendous. It grows and spreads like a wildfire. The world is in need of forgiveness and healing that only Christ Himself can give through those willing to humble themselves and allow Christ to heal the hurt and pain caused by others. We must stop viewing ourselves as the victims and stop requiring others to pay a pound of flesh for their wrongs toward us. That is the only way out of the bitterness prison.

Holding onto bitterness encourages sin and prevents growth in our spiritual lives. This is why people who hold onto bitterness never mature in their faith. Bitterness damages their relationships with God and others. It creates disharmony. Finally, it hurts their testimonies as believers in Christ.

Reflection

1. Is there anyone against whom you hold an offense?
   Describe the situation.

2. On what basis can you continue holding your offense in light of the above Scriptures?

3. Are you willing to appropriate God's grace to forgive them and allow bitterness to be removed from your life?

   Schedule a time to seek out any individuals who fit this description in your life.

Conclusion

"Brokenness is the beginning of humility and the place where we find the nature of Christ. There is only one way for Christians to come back to the place of right standing with the Lord Jesus. God uses most for His glory in those people and things which are most perfectly broken. The sacrifices He accepts are broken and contrite hearts. It was the breaking down of Jacob's natural strength at Peniel that got him where God could clothe him with spiritual power. It was breaking the surface of the rock at Horeb, by the stroke of Moses' rod, that let out the cool water to thirsty people.

It was when the three hundred elect soldiers under Gideon broke their pitchers, a type of breaking themselves, that the hidden lights shone forth to the consternation of their adversaries. It was when the poor widow broke the seal of the little pot of oil, and poured it forth, that God multiplied it to pay her debts and supply means of support.

It was when Esther risked her life and broke through the rigid etiquette of a heathen court, that she obtained favor to rescue her people from death. It was when Jesus took the five loaves and broke them, that the bread was multiplied in the very act of breaking, sufficient to feed five thousand. It was when Mary broke her beautiful alabaster box, rendering it henceforth useless, that the pent-up perfume filled the house. It was when Jesus allowed His precious body to be broken to pieces by thorns and spear, that His inner life was poured out, like a crystal ocean, for thirsty sinners to drink and live.

It is when a beautiful grain of corn is broken up in the earth by DEATH, that His inner heart sprouts forth and bears hundreds of other grains. And thus, on and on, through history, and all biography, and all vegetation, and all spiritual life, God must have BROKEN THINGS.

Those who are broken in wealth, and broken in self-will, and broken in their ambitions, and broken in their beautiful ideals, and broken in worldly reputation, and broken in their affections, and broken oftentimes in health; those who are despised and seem utterly forlorn and helpless, the Holy Ghost is seizing upon, and using for God's glory. 'The lame take the prey,' Isaiah tells us." [11]

A CALL TO RESTORATION

This book has covered a period of two-and-a-half years, from March of 1994 to September of 1996. This is a stopping point, but certainly not a completion point. I am a person, like you, who is still a "work-in-progress". We will all be this way until the Lord returns or we go to be with Him. I often tell people it has been the most difficult, but the best period of my life. Difficult, for obvious reasons. Best, because of what I have learned, experienced and seen God do in the midst of these difficulties. I've learned it has been God's strategic mercy in my life. That may genuinely sound like pie in the sky for you to believe. But I can tell you, I am truly touched by the mercy and love of God as a result of what I now know from these experiences. I would go through them again if it meant knowing and experiencing the call of God on my life the way I now can see it.

Over the two and a half year period God allowed me to experience many personal and business disappointments that were the catalyst God used to demonstrate His sovereign work in my life. These events brought me to a point of willingness to fulfill the purposes He had prepared in advance. An overriding truth that I discovered was that God is, in fact, a very omnipotent God. The difficult events that took place were all a part of God's perfect plan — even my failures. I realized first-hand when God said in Psalm 139 that He knew me from the foundations of the world, and that the events of my life are all orchestrated for the purposes He wants to accomplish through me. I have discovered that all of my life experiences that led up to this particular period were important in order to frame my life. This realization allowed me to be a willing participant in His larger plan to positively impact the lives of others through the lessons He was teaching me (see 2 Corinthians 1:3,4). This is one of the comforting lessons I hope you will take away from this book. God has a specific calling and purpose for each of us.

There were many specific lessons learned throughout the period I have touched upon in this book. There were many crossroads where choices had to be made. I hope you could see these times clearly throughout the book and were encouraged as you experience your own pilgrimage with God. At each crossroad a question of obedience would determine if I would follow feelings, hurts, and bitterness, or obedience even if that didn't always produce a seemingly positive outcome. Each of these choices would ultimately determine the path God would take me to next.

One such painful realization was that as a business owner most of my adult life I had never learned what it meant to belong to others, nor had I ever known what it really meant to give myself to others. I grew up with a very independent view of life that demonstrated a willingness to interact with others, but not involve myself emotionally. One of the older men in one of my men's groups made a profound statement as it relates to our ability to "belong" to others. He said, "When someone else's child comes to sit in my lap, I take that as a sign that the level of relationship to that family has grown to a deeper level of trust and belonging." I had few of these kinds of relationships with another family's children until I began in this process. It wasn't that I was not willing, it had just never been modeled, so I didn't know what it looked like. I grew up thinking my way of relating was like everyone else's. In one sense, I was right. But I discovered there is a better and more fulfilling way to relate to others.

Through these two-and-a-half years I learned that God uses individuals in our lives to be the instruments of change that He desires. For me, I have seen this truth incredibly lived out. I can truly testify to Proverbs 13:20 which states, *"He who walks with the wise grows wise, but a companion of fools suffers harm."* God sent key individuals to me that have impacted my life significantly. God even reinforced this knowledge by leading me to scriptures at strategic times, such as on June 4, 1995, when I read these verses from Isaiah 30:20-23:

> *Although the Lord gives you the bread of adversity and the water of affliction, your teachers will be hidden no more; with your own eyes you will see them. Whether you turn to the right or to the left, your ears will hear a voice behind you, saying, "This is the way; walk in it." Then you will defile your idols overlaid with silver and your images covered with gold; you will throw them away like a menstrual cloth and say to them, "Away with you!" He will also send you rain for the seed you sow in the ground, and the food that comes from the land will be rich and plentiful. In that day your cattle will graze in broad meadows* (Isaiah 30:20-23).

This Scripture was meaningful because I had been questioning whether the people around me at this time were truly sent by God, or were distractions from what God was really trying to do in my life. I also was learning important lessons about the wrong priorities that I had set in the past. I felt God was initiating something significant about a year after the separation from my wife when I met a couple who would ultimately impact my life greatly. They showed up at the most strategic time. I wasn't looking for them, but through God's omnipotent mercy, He directed these individuals to me when He decided I needed them at strategic crossroads. Unfortunately, I did not know what further pain and "crisis of belief" periods I would encounter as a result of their friendship.

I realized nine months after knowing Mike Dowgiewicz that God had, in fact, sent one of His generals in the kingdom from New England to handle a real problem child down in Atlanta. One of Mike's favorite verses was Psalm 17:14:" *O Lord, by Your hand save me from such men, from men of this world whose reward is in this life.*" God gave me a picture of my relationship with Mike. The picture was a pole vaulter who was vaulting over a spiritual crossbar. Every time I reached one level of the crossbar Mike looked at me smilingly and raised the spiritual crossbar. I don't think he consciously did this. There were so many gut-wrenching times of discouragement and crises of belief. Mike's love for Jesus and disregard for the things of this world created a real problem for me. I have never known anyone like Mike and his wife Sue. But God knew the kind of individuals that were required to bring about the changes that He wanted to make in me for the sake of the calling He was placing on my life.

In June 1995 I had to take a trip to Seattle, Washington for business and personal ministry reasons. On that trip I attended a church for three nightly meetings. On the second night I was prayed for by three individuals within this church who had the spiritual gift of prophecy. I did not know the individuals who prayed for me, nor had they ever met me.

As a result of what I had been learning through the trials of these many months, I began sharing these truths with other men. My increasing transparency and vulnerability with others became a source of blessing for some, and difficult for others. The two prophecies below were shared with me during these meetings and helped demonstrate God's confirming hand in what He was and is doing in my life.

The Lord is pleased with you. You've been very open and vulnerable with people — almost to a fault at times. But God is going to use that in the lives of others in a greater way. You will need to discern when is the appropriate time to be open and vulnerable. This will be a source of pain in some situations because of your willingness to be vulnerable. Not everyone will be comfortable with your level of openness and transparency. June, 1995

Vulnerability has not always been a characteristic of my life. I thank the Lord Jesus Christ for leading me into this new level of walking with Him. The second prophecy was a bit more difficult to understand, but I believe was fulfilled at the end of the two and a half year period.

I see a series of fruit trees with fruit on them. The first row was small. Over your life you have row upon row of trees, each row larger and larger. You have been eating of this fruit over your lifetime. There is one more large tree that you have yet to eat from before the Lord is going to take you into a new level of relationship with Him that you have never known before. June, 1995

Exactly two and a half years after this process started the most devastating event yet took place in my life. I am not at liberty to share this event in print, but it served to bring me to a point of appropriating God's grace in ways I had not needed until that point. I think this was the large tree God was speaking of.

Perhaps you, the reader, are not accustomed to prophecy. I realize that may be the case for some. However, I must testify to what I have seen and heard as it relates to God's work in my life (see John 3:11, Acts 4:19). My church experience has been very broad over the twenty-three years that I have been a Christian. I was saved in a Southern Baptist Church. Throughout the years I have been involved in many different denominational churches — from evangelical to Pentecostal. Early in my Christian experience I adopted a view that I wanted everything the Lord had for me. I realized that the experiences with many different denominational churches have allowed me to focus on the key issues of the Christian faith, while considering those doctrines that make denominations different to be insignificant to the overall purposes God was to accomplish in my life and the lives of other people. This philosophy has served me well without sacrificing my basic foundational beliefs. Someone once said "doctrine is what you're willing to die for;" The foundations of my faith, Jesus Christ, is all that is worth dying for; the various doctrinal factions, I learned, are not.

After meeting Mike and Sue, I realized that what God had started doing in my life even before I ever met them was, in part, fulfilling a message and calling that God had given them to share while they were in Israel in 1993 and 1994. A global movement of God is occurring at this time. I believe that I, and many other business people are part of this movement of God. Throughout the world today God is calling the Jewish people to the land of Israel and is in the process of restoring the Hebraic principles of the early church that made it a powerful force during its time. This restoration movement is trickling down to individuals like me, who have discovered something missing in their organized church experience. There was a reason the early church experienced power in the first century and why so many were willing to die for their faith. That is not a part of many Christians' church experience today.

Why aren't there more non-Christians in the United States attracted to Christianity today? The answer is quite simple. It is the same reason why many of us begin to lose our excitement in walking with God. We are often devoted, committed Christians who serve God, but do not SEE God at work in and around us. Many non-Christians see "Christians" living in their own strength, but they do not see anything happening that can only be explained as the *activity of God*. That is because they often are not attempting things that only God can do. They are not attracted to live for Christ because they cannot see Him at work in accomplishing things *only He can do*. So, in order for others to be drawn to Jesus we must return to the principles that guided the early Church which demonstrated the reality of a miracle-working God. The reality of a miracle-working God caused them to be witnesses to what they had seen and heard:

> *Truly, truly, I say to you, we speak that which we know, and bear witness of that which we have seen; and you do not receive our witness* (John 3:11).

> *But Peter and John answered and said to them, "Whether it is right in the sight of God to give heed to you rather than to God, you be the judge; for we cannot stop speaking what we have seen and heard* (Acts 4:19,20).

> *...what we have seen and heard we proclaim to you also, that you also may have fellowship with us...*(1 John 1:3).

The apostle Paul knew that it wasn't just his message that had affected people: *"My message and my preaching were not with wise and persuasive words, <u>but with a demonstration of the Spirit's power,</u> so that your faith might not rest on men's wisdom, but on God's power"* (1 Corinthians 2:4,5 emphasis added). Research shows that by the third century many anti-Semitic writings and practices had entered the church through the teachings and philosophical influences of converted Greek philosophers. Their attempts to reconcile Plato and Christianity replaced the Hebraic foundations that had strengthened the Early Church. The following short comparison illustrates the differences between the Hebraic and Greek approaches to living out the Word of God.

HEBRAIC	GREEK
Active - appeals to the heart	*Cognitive* - appeals to theintellect
Process Oriented	*Program Oriented*
• Emphasizes direct participation	• Heavy program emphasis
• Emphasizes age and wisdom Role modeling, mentoring, and discipleship indispensable	• Emphasizes education
	• Relies on speaking skills, oratory, programmed materials, information conveyance
• Leadership by personal example	
• Character of leaders essential	• Leader's personal life less essential
• Personal relationships essential	• Personal relationships optional
Biblical Application	*Biblical Application*
• Doers of the Word	• Belief without cost to self
• Bible — reality that must be confronted	• Bible — data that must be taught
	• Focus on rules — do's and don'ts
• Goal — develop Christlikeness	• Emphasizes distinct denominations
Ministry Activity	*Ministry Activity*
• Small intimate groups	• Large impersonal groups
• Leader as facilitator	• Leader-directed and controlled
• Cooperative, participatory planning	• Organizational roles important
• Spiritual gifts shared	• Acquisition of knowledge emphasized
• Frequent scheduled and unscheduled gatherings	• Reliance on scheduled gatherings

continued...

Fruit	Fruit
• Love, acceptance, forgiveness	• Mutual toleration
• Transparency encouraged	• Tranparency discouraged
• Active participation	• Passivity and lethargy
• "How you serve" vital	• "What you know" vital
• Each believer trained to serve	• Trained professionals utilized
• Produces mature believers	• Produces spectators

I realized that I was a product of the Greek influenced church. I had gained a great deal of head knowledge, but was bearing little fruit from that knowledge. As a result of what God was taking me through, I realized that God was restoring a more Hebraic walk with God without realizing it until I came into contact with Mike and Sue. Much of my walk with God could be characterized by the column on the right.

Someone once said, "Nobody cares what you know until they know that you care." Caring was a vital element of the early church. Mike helped me understand how the early Hebraic church operated and how God wants to restore the principles of the early church that had made it a powerful force in the world. As we enter the last days, more and more of God's people are becoming aware of a movement toward what the early church was built upon. This message is reawakening believers in various parts of the United States.

In the early church the primary relational focus was each individual's personal walk with Jesus. After that, Marriage was sacred and was representative of Jesus' relationship to His church. In other words, the early church felt, "If you want to know my relationship with Jesus, then watch how I treat my spouse." How many of us can say that today? I knew I had failed in my own marital relationship and that I was just one of many others who are going down the same road. With the failures of over fifty percent of marriages that are performed in a church setting, it does not say much for the strength of our families or for the effectiveness of churches today. The Hebraic language did not have a word for "bachelor." It was more important for a Hebrew man to find a wife before he pursued any other calling. On every Sabbath in the Jewish home, the father would read Proverbs 31:10-31 aloud.

> *A wife of noble character who can find? She is worth far more than rubies. Her husband has full confidence in her and lacks nothing of value. She selects wool and flax and works with eager hands. She is like the merchant ships, bringing her food from afar. She gets up while it is still dark; she provides food for her family and portions for her servant girls. She considers a field and buys it; out of her earnings she plants a vineyard. She sets about her work vigorously; her arms are strong for her tasks. She sees that her trading is profitable, and her lamp does not go out at night. In her hand she holds the distaff and grasps the spindle with her fingers* (Proverbs 31:10-19).

This custom recognized the importance of the wife in the home. The father was the priest in the home, and was responsible for the spiritual nurturing of the family.

The following diagram represents the emphasis of the early church.

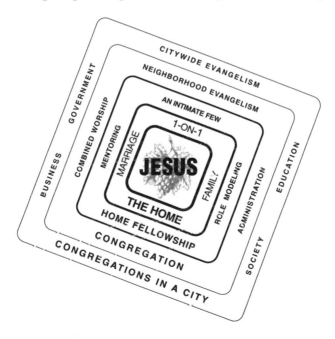

The early church understood that the most important relationship was with Jesus. Next, the marriage and home were the most important. The father was the priest in the home. The home fellowship was the next level of caring outside the home. Finally, it was not until one got to the fourth level out that a congregational gathering took place. Today's church tries to achieve the first four levels at the congregational level.

The Home Fellowship was the next level of relationship for the early church. These relationships were deep, caring, load-bearing relationships. It was not until these first relationships were healthy and vibrant that the Congregational meeting took place. These emphases are also paramount to living out a healthy walk with God in Business. When these priorities are not being lived out symptoms of greater problems begin arising in each of the above levels. Today we find the congregational aspect of our church experience trying to fulfill the first three levels of relationship. Meanwhile, thousands upon thousands of once church-going Christians have left the organized church because their needs are not being met due to the programmatic structure of today's church. The breakdown of these key relationships is a primary reason why the church has lost its first century power.[12] (Mike and Sue Dowgiewicz have detailed the restoration movement in their book, *Restoring The Early Church*, Aslan Group Publishing).

I realized that my life physically represented the breakdown of the Greek system. I had to restore the foundations of my life to the priorities that God wanted. A lot of ground had been lost. It was not easy restoring many of these areas. I faced many forks in the road. My relationship with Jesus had become programmatic and stagnant. I had allowed wrong priorities to come into that most important relationship, Jesus. That eventually led to wrong choices for myself, my marriage, and my family. My relationship with my wife deteriorated to the point that we were separated for over two years. I was committed to trying to save the relationship, but she eventually filed for divorce after sixteen years of marriage. My business was affected and nearly went under because of some of these wrong priorities. I had few deep, caring relationships which allowed me to belong to others or others to belong to me up until this time. I had been lost in the church system. And my wife, family, business and key relationships had become the casualties.

My story also reveals how God began to implement His greater purposes as one of many "Josephs" God is raising up all around the world right now. Christian men and women business owners and leaders are being called to a significant movement of God throughout the world that will be part of these last days. These men and women are being "recruited" through a bootcamp that often involves their own form of imprisonment that is designed to bring them to a level of relationship they never knew existed. These hardships are the refining fire of preparation for business people in these last days. If you are a business person and you have experienced any crisis events in your personal and business life, I have written another book entitled *Prosperity and The Christian In Business* that details this trend among Christian business people. Many Christian leaders have affirmed that God is going to do a significant work within Christian business people in these last days. It is no accident that God led me to start Aslan Group Publishing in November of 1995 to share many of these truths.

Then, in July, 1996 God led me and some other business people to begin a magazine called *Christians In Business*, established to help Christians experience Christ in their own marketplace. I wasn't looking to go into publishing, but His guiding hand was clear that this was His plan.

May God richly bless you as you seek to reflect His character and purposes in your life.

Verses on Suffering
Addendum A

2 Cor. 1:6 *If we are distressed, it is for your comfort and salvation; if we are comforted, it is for your comfort, which produces in you patient endurance of the same sufferings we suffer.*

Phil. 1:29 *For it has been granted to you on behalf of Christ not only to believe on Him, but also to suffer for Him.*

1 Pet. 1:6 *In this you greatly rejoice, though now for a little while you may have had to suffer grief in all kinds of trials.*

1 Pet. 2:20 *But how is it to your credit if you receive a beating for doing wrong and endure it? But if you suffer for doing good and you endure it, this is commendable before God.*

1 Pet. 3:14 *But even if you should suffer for what is right, you are blessed. Do not fear what they fear; do not be frightened.*

1 Pet. 3:17 *It is better, if it is God's will, to suffer for doing good than for doing evil.*

1 Pet. 4:15 *If you suffer, it should not be as a murderer or thief or any other kind of criminal, or even as a meddler. However, if you suffer as a Christian, do not be ashamed, but praise God that you bear that name.*

1 Pet. 4:19 *So then, those who suffer according to God's will should commit themselves to their faithful Creator and continue to do good.*

Rev. 2:10 *Do not be afraid of what you are about to suffer. I tell you, the devil will put some of you in prison to test you, and you will suffer persecution for ten days. Be faithful, even to the point of death, and I will give you the crown of life.*

Acts 5:41   *The apostles left the Sanhedrin, rejoicing because they had been counted worthy of suffering disgrace for the Name.*

Acts 7:11   *Then a famine struck all Egypt and Canaan, bringing great suffering, and our fathers could not find food.*

Rom. 5:3   *Not only so, but we also rejoice in our sufferings, because we know that suffering produces perseverance.*

1 Ths. 1:6   *You became imitators of us and of the Lord; in spite of severe suffering, you welcomed the message with the joy given by the Holy Spirit.*

2 Ths. 1:5   *All this is evidence that God's judgment is right, and as a result you will be counted worthy of the kingdom of God, for which you are suffering.*

2 Tim. 1:8   *So do not be ashamed to testify about our Lord, or ashamed of me his prisoner. But join with me in suffering for the gospel, by the power of God.*

2 Tim. 1:12   *That is why I am suffering as I am. Yet I am not ashamed, because I know whom I have believed, and am convinced that He is able to guard what I have entrusted to Him for that day.*

2 Tim. 2:9   *. . . for which I am suffering even to the point of being chained like a criminal. But God's word is not chained.*

Heb. 2:10   *In bringing many sons to glory, it was fitting that God, for Whom and through Whom everything exists, should make the author of their salvation perfect through suffering.*

Heb. 10:32   *Remember those earlier days after you had received the light, when you stood your ground in a great contest in the face of suffering.*

Heb. 13:3   *Remember those in prison as if you were their fellow prisoners, and those who are mistreated as if you yourselves were suffering.*

James 5:10   *Brothers, as an example of patience in the face of suffering, take the prophets who spoke in the name of the Lord.*

1 Pet. 2:19   *For it is commendable if a man bears up under the pain of unjust suffering because he is conscious of God.*

Rev. 1:9   *I, John, your brother and companion in the suffering and kingdom and patient endurance that are ours in Jesus, was on the island of Patmos because of the word of God and the testimony of Jesus.*

Bibliography

1. *The Lies We Believe,* Dr. Chris Thurman, excerpt from audio-cassette discussion with Christian Counselors.

2. *The Three Battlegrounds,* Frances Frangipane, Arrow Publications, p. 71,72.

3. *The Problem With Pain,* C.S. Lewis, (New York: Macmillan, 1966), p.

4. *More Than Conquerors,* John Woodbridge, Moody Press, p. 349.

5. *Hinds' Feet On High Places,* Hannah Hurnard, Tyndale Publishing, p.121.

6 . *Hinds' Feet On High Places*, Hannah Hurnard, Tyndale Publishing, p. 240-242.

7. *Adversity,* Charles Stanley, Oliver-Nelson books, p. 98.

8. *The Three Battlegrounds*, Francis Frangipane, Arrow Publications, p. 41,42

9. *None of These Diseases*, S.I. McMillen, Spire Books, 1968, pp. 69-72.

10. Institute in Basic Life Principles workbook, p.82.

11. *Streams in the Desert*, Daybreak Books, Volume 1, p. 318

12. *Restoring The Early Church,* Mike and Sue Dowgiewicz, Aslan Group Publishing, p.285

Additional Resources Available From

ASLAN GROUP
P U B L I S H I N G

Books:	Product #	Unit Price*
• Demolishing Strongholds	336	$15.00
• Restoring The Early Church	732	$14.95
• Adversity and Pain: *The Gifts That Nobody Wants*	238	$7.95
• The Five Fallacies of The Purposes of Money	348	$4.95

Booklets:

• The Restoration of Spiritual Gifts *Knowing Your Spiritual Gifts and* *Cooperating with the Gifts of Others to* *Win the War Against the Powers of Darkness*	737	Call for Price
• The Christian *Halakhah*s of the Bible *Displaying Your Love for Jesus* *Through the Way You Apply His Word*	425	Call for Price

Magazine:

• *Christians IN Business* magazine subscription Call 1-888-242-4412 to subscribe		1 Year $26.95 2 Years $29.95

*Volume Discounts Available:
10 or more books - 10% off • 20 or more books - 20% off

Available at your local Christian bookstore or call:
1-800-311-2103 (extension 107)

Aslan Group Publishing
3595 Webb Bridge Rd.   Alpharetta, GA 30202
770/442-1003   Toll Free 1-800/311-2103   FAX 770/442-1844
e-mail: Hillman.aslangroup@mindspring.com